THE BOOK OF COP
A TESTAMENT TO POLICING THAT WORKS

BY STEPHEN TABELING AND STEPHEN JANIS

Cover and Interior Design: Jocelyn Dombroski
Editing: Taya Graham and Ophelia Moonrose
Published by Baltimore True crime
Contact: novelzine@gmail.com

I dedicate this book to Sgt. Robert Holland, who recently passed. He was an outstanding police partner who gave me guidance and insight throughout my rookie years and beyond. He was a steadfast friend, and I appreciate all the insight he shared with me during his life on how to be both a good cop and a decent human being.

To Jerry
Steve Tabeling
10/24/7

ACKNOWLEDGEMENTS

This book is not just a chronicle of my career as a cop, but also a humble recognition of the incredible people I worked with on the cases recounted in the proceeding pages. The judges, prosecutors, and police officers listed below represent the best practitioners, protectors, and enforcers of the law I have ever met.

Each and every one of the people on this list personifies the true meaning of the term "public servant." They taught me how to be a better cop, and also how to remain a decent human being amidst the chaos and corruption that comes with investigating crime in Baltimore.

Thus I hope by acknowledging them here, I pay tribute to their service to both the community of Baltimore and the laws they fought to uphold to protect it.

The Honorable Charles E. Moylan Jr.
The Honorable Joseph Murphy
The Honorable Peter Ward
The Honorable Thomas Bollinger
The Honorable Robert Dugan
Assistant State Prosecutor Stephen R. Tully
Assistant State's Attorney Marianne Willin-Saar
Captain James J. Cadden
Major John Reintzel
Lieutenant Leander "Bunny" Nevin
Sergeant Rosario Buzzuro
Detective Steve Danko
Detective Timothy Timmons
Detective Jerome Johnson
Detective Nicholas Giangrasso
Detective Howard Corbin
Officer James Brennan
Sgt. Robert Holland

"I've looked into the mirror, I've turned the spotlight on myself. I've tried to question my beliefs, and most of all re-examine the whole idea of what it means to be a cop. For want of a better term, I would call this the Book of Cop. The ugly liturgy of policing, a compilation of meager truths and bitter pills, some swallowed, some not."

You Can't Stop Murder:
Truths About Policing in Baltimore and Beyond

A NOTE ABOUT THE METHODOLOGY
OF THIS BOOK

The Book of Cop is not intended to be a chronology of my career. Instead, I selected the most vexing cases I investigated as a jumping-off point for considering and reexamining why we police at all.

Each case raises fundamental questions about the most difficult issues confronting contemporary law enforcement today. Each chapter contains both the details of the events as I recall them, along with discussion about the topic most relevant to the case itself: the law and how to apply it.

But there are also essays on the peculiarities and contradictions of applying the law to people. A task that becomes even more complicated when a cop confronts the most extreme types of human behavior.

In a sense, this book, like my previous work, is a detective novel. I have not just solely focused on the practical side of solving crimes. The enigmatic riddle I try to unravel is why people commit irrational acts with regularity? To answer the question: What prompts the random act of violence, the horrible murder, the most extreme examples of human behavior? And more importantly, how should law enforcement respond? How might we survive human savagery and misbehavior and not succumb to it ourselves? And fundamentally, should there be limits to how far we as a society are willing to go to be safe?

Any good detective knows these are often the most difficult questions that populate a crime scene. After all, crime is a human endeavor, not a science or profession; we just turn it into one on the back end. And any detective will tell you, a terrifying fact cops face while investigating a heinous crime is just how human it is.

One note about the cases described here, in some instances, I have changed the sequence of events, concealed the names of people involved, or altered minor details of how the case unfolded. My reason for doing so is twofold: to provide the people who suffered through these crimes a semblance of anonymity, and to allow some flexibility in discussing how I felt about what happened both then and now.

While the tales told in this book focus on acts that happened long ago, as an investigator I always mindful about offering opinions on the cases I worked. Thus I have tried to be careful how the narrative of each case is constructed to preserve some privacy and dignity for both the victims and the men and women I worked with to solve them. All of these alterations are subtle and do not affect the substance of the stories recounted herein.

TABLE OF CONTENTS

CHAPTER ONE:
POLICING THE MYTH

The year 2017 is undoubtedly a tough time to be a cop.

The debate over how and even why we police has never been more fraught. Police involved shootings caught on video make headlines and prompt national outrage. The perception that law enforcement treats African-Americans differently has become ingrained in our national consciousness. And the symbol of police as freestyle drug warriors has so infiltrated both popular culture and the narrative of urban policing, that the old school cop in uniform on the beat seems like a relic from a long-forgotten era of an entirely different profession.

But there s something else that has taken hold of policing that bothers me even more. A familiar narrative that continues to transform the profession into something akin to a religion, not a public service. A characterization of the calling that probably has more to do with the aforementioned problems than tactics, botched reform, or any other prescription being debated in the present.

Let me explain.

I grew up in southeast Baltimore in the 1930s. A hardscrabble stretch of pavement forged by a polyglot of immigrants. It was blue collar Baltimore to the core.

Jobs were scarce, my education limited, and my parents worked hard to provide for us. The neighborhood was tight knit, but the truth is, it was a land of limited options.

So after marrying the love of my life, Honey, and driving a bus for a few years, I decided to become a cop. It was a decision that changed my life.

During my 60-plus-years in law enforcement, I worked every beat from burglary to homicide. I was the first internal affairs investigator for the Baltimore City Police Department. I trained officers on the law at the academy. I even held the title of chief of police in a small town on Maryland's eastern shore called Salisbury.

Along the way, I picked up my undergraduate diploma and a couple of graduate degrees in psychology and public administration.

But when I think back about all that I've learned, I feel like something is missing. Like I have been remiss in making one final contribution to the profession that transformed my life and made me the man I am today.

There's a bit of regret, and even second thoughts–not about becoming a cop, but what it means to be one. Someone needs to offer a reasonable explanation for both how and why we police. To answer the complex question of why we hire men and women to immerse themselves in chaos. To acknowledge and explain the nitty-gritty of what it's like being a cop on the street where respect for human life is sometimes in short supply.

I've already written one book: *You Can t Stop Murder*. In that book I already argued that contemporary policing needs a comprehensive overhaul. Not a return to the old ways, but a reexamination of the entire profession. That officers need to reacquaint themselves with the law. To practice law enforcement within the legal guidelines and formal rules designed to govern it and in doing so make it more effective.

I explicated this premise through the prism of the most dramatic cases of my career.

From the day a crazed gunman stormed city hall and murdered a councilman, to the execution-style slaying of a state delegate after the feds charged him with drug dealing.

I recounted the day a 17-year-old sniper launched a vicious attack on the corner of Lombard and Carey Streets in Southwest Baltimore, shooting seven cops in a matter of hours. And I told the story of how I had the unpleasant task of investigating a death threat against a former police commissioner.

All these stories were told within the framework of my simple thesis–that the law means something. That it is constructed with thoughtfulness and consideration of not just corralling lawbreakers or executing drug busts, but to create a just, peaceful, and orderly society.

But *The Book of the Cop* is going to be different. It will offer a critique of a problem I failed to address in *You Can't Stop Murder*. A question that is at the heart of the heated debate going on right now regarding policing. Something that we need to thoroughly examine if we want to fix it. A philosophical debate that may be too far afield for a cop book, but one I think is absolutely necessary to save policing from itself:

Why do we police at all? Why bother? Why do we need it?

Questions that perhaps seems too obvious to require an answer, but are worth exploring.

I would argue that of course, we need police. We need cops because people break the law. Because every day in this country someone chooses to murder, rape/steal, and otherwise wreak havoc. Because someone has to patrol the streets and answer calls of distress. Because somebody has to do the dirty work of a society long accustomed to having a police car just a phone call away. Policing is simply embedded in the fabric of our lives, but that's not always been the case.

It may seem hard to believe, but of all the branches of municipal government policing was, in fact, the last to emerge. In the 19th century, the task of law enforcement was usually vested in a constabulary, an agency akin to a sheriff that could jail and confiscate property for example, but not actively enforce the law.

It was only when British Prime Minister Sir Robert Peele decided the United Kingdom needed a more proactive way to maintain a civil society that the concept of modern policing was born.

Peele's idea, creating a professional cadre of active law enforcers was met with not just skepticism, but outright hostility. British citizens were afraid that this so-called police force would turn into a modern day Praetorian Guard, a group of armed and dangerous soldiers loyal to the politicians who employed them, but with little concern for the populace, they were tasked to serve.

To address these fears, Peele was alleged to have created a set of principles which became the foundation of modern policing. Still known to this day as the Peelian Principles, it proffers a set of checks and balances on the power of police to enforce the law in a community fearful professional law enforcement would become just another branch of the military. I won't recount them all now, but in general, outlined a very robust and in my opinion ingenious philosophy: to police effectively, you must be impartial, judicious, transparent, and above all, do so with the full consent of the people.

Which brings me to this book, *The Book of Cop*. In it, I want to re-examine this idea. Not just a set of principles per se, but what they mean on the streets. How a split-second decision to use force in the heat of the moment can have devastating consequences for both the officer and the public, but still, must be justified. How the politics of crime stats and public perception can influence policy and strategy, to the extent the cops are asked to make useless arrests and unproductive stops. How our current estrangement from the public has dulled our ability to communicate with the community we serve.

In other words, I want to get inside the profession that can at times seem mystifying, beguiling, frustratingly insular, and unnecessarily opaque. I want to offer you, the reader, a first-hand perspective on the uncertainty, terror, and downright absurdity that comprises the profession of policing I want to cross the thin blue line, rip it up and throw it away.

The point is, I want to build a bridge of understanding between the people who the wear the badge, and the people we serve. And in doing so, construct a better model of policing based on the realities of the job, not the rhetoric of politics.And I won't do this with an amalgam of bullet points or excerpts from an old training manual. Instead, like my last book, I will instruct by example. Or better yet, reveal strategies and methods through the tales of the cases, crimes, and corruption I have investigated and witnessed first-hand. In a sense, I will mine the past for insight into the present. And more importantly, offer a detailed account of how all the admixture of uncertainty and fear can undermine even the best cop.

But tactics and casework is not the only aspect of policing I want to address. I also will be laying out a critique of the way we talk about policing, and why it needs to change. A sort of pathology that has become pervasive in the lexicon of both law enforcement advocates and politicians alike. A particular form of laudatory rhetoric, which has come to define policing in a manner that I think is unhealthy for our profession.

I call it, for lack of a better phrase, the mythologizing of the trade. The constant stream of laudatory rhetoric proffered by politicians and union officials that cops are heroes, risking their lives daily, men and women prepared to sacrifice it all for the benefit of the community.

This is all true. I've witnessed it. I ve seen both remarkable courage and exemplary bravery. And I too have stared down the barrel of one too many hostile guns, disarmed knife-wielding maniacs, and even shot and killed a man in West Baltimore alley when he drew a weapon and left me no choice.

But while I have watched countless acts of courage by my fellow officers and recognize that every single cop has the duty to put themselves at risk every day; I fear the constant drumbeat of this defensive rhetoric in the form of rote praise not only diminishes the real value of it but only deepens the entrenched instincts of law enforcement to insulate itself from accountability and public discourse.

A good example of this over-the-top rhetoric is what is known as the 'bad apples theory.' It's become almost boilerplate language embedded in the repertoire of politicians when they talk about policing. Inevitably at some point during every public discussion about a particular cop's misdeeds, the speaker will qualify his or her remarks with a statement that "the majority of our officers are hard working, honest cops."

The implication, of course, is that any criticism of policing, and how we do our jobs, is no criticism at all. That behind the blue line is a group of unimpeachable moral actors. People who are not just heroes, but nearly superhuman. A group entirely distinct from the bad cop who strayed.

I understand the impulse. Criticizing cops is tough. Not just because of the difficulty of the job, but because our political power has become a sort centripetal force. Police unions, particularly in cities like Baltimore with proportionately large departments, have unparalleled influence.

They dictate work schedules, street tactics, and even have a pretty big say in who gets to sit in the commissioner's chair. For all intents and purposes, our profession has become a veritable political institution with a seat at almost every civic table.

But that's just part of the problem. Rooted in the confluence of politics, money, and power that has transformed the profession into a special interest of vast influence is a single-minded resistance to introspection and self-critique that has done more to damage policing than all the botched policies and flawed strategies. The idea that we are somehow inscrutable. That police are above the fray of criticism and accountability. That we will do anything to protect our own against rightful demands of the public to weigh in.

And it all starts with mythologizing.

That sense of invulnerability might feel good in the short run, but fosters bad habits and poor strategic thinking over time. It insulates the profession and prevents frank discussions on how policing can be improved and reformed. It promotes an atmosphere of inwardness which is the polar opposite of the Peelian principles, and worst of all, it takes the human being out of the uniform and creates a public image that becomes easy even harder to empathize with and easy to spurn.

Bear in mind I understand there is a strong, albeit oppositely situated mythologizing evolving in the public consciousness. The idea that policing is inherently corrupt. That cops are crooks. That the thin blue line is really just a mass collusion to keep all the nasty, dirty business of policing behind an impenetrable curtain. I watch and read these sentiments both on television and in newspapers every day. That we are indeed a Praetorian guard, more interested in self-preservation than serving the public.

It's a rhetorical divide that only strengthens the imperative for both sides to dig in. And that's not healthy for anyone, cops or the citizenry.

Like I've already stated, police make life or death decisions on a daily basis. We carry guns. We have the power and the choice to take away someone's freedom. We can charge people with crimes. Decisions that are unpopular, and sometimes not always explicable. A fraught and occasionally painful process that sometimes requires defending and explanations that often seem inadequate.

But what the rhetoric on both sides misses is complexity, that is the self-consciousness of human duality that comes with being the instant arbiter of the law. The imperative of uncertainty you absorb while answering a call that someone has a gun, a suspicious person is loitering on a residential street, or that a burglary is in progress. The constant need to respond to uncertainty, chaos, and the threat of violence. The seemingly endless continuum of self-destructive behavior that we as a community have decided must be addressed, if not contained by police.

I think it's a hard perspective to understand if you haven't done it. If you haven't been the beat cop driving the patrol car when the call comes over the radio that an active shooter is tearing up a block in West Baltimore. Or the supervisor who receives word a bullet-ridden body of a State Delegate has been found in the bowels of an abandoned parking garage. Or bounded up a flight of stairs answering a domestic call and not knowing what's on the other side of the door, a man with a knife or a gun who may or may not be willing to use it. It's hard to understand if you haven't been there.

Which is why I'm writing this book. Because I believe the gap in understanding between cops and civilians is our fault. Connecting to the public, as Peele made clear, is our responsibility. We, the police, have to reach out and tell our stories. Not just tales of drama and danger, but narratives which explain the complex forces that make the job difficult, risky, but necessary.

Stories which reveal the wild and unwieldy spectrum of human behavior we confront on a daily basis, and how we try to cope with it in the most humane way possible. The onus is on us to explain it, because if we don t, nobody will. And if we don t try, the gulf that divides us now will only widen.

So, in the ensuing chapters, I will humbly attempt to help you understand all the vexing realities of policing. How the job can be ennobling and satisfying, but also traumatic and troubling. How being a police officer requires creativity and empathy, not just the willingness to point and shoot. Why cops are human beings, in some sense irrevocably altered by the task of confronting the worst aspects of human nature one day, and the most trivial and seemingly pointless conflicts people can conjure the next.

It is the mixture of the ridiculous and the terrifying, the mundane and the mortifying, that I will explore without pretense or censorship. A liturgy of truisms about the profession of policing which I hope will help you understand us. A bridge between the police and the public built upon my experience and understanding of the job. A small token of appreciation to the people I served from a man who gladly did just that with both the pride and passion. A final missive to my community on how policing can make the world a happier, safer place.

CHAPTER TWO:
THE STREETS ARE MEANT FOR WALKING

Pennsylvania Avenue was dark when the call box lit up. The recently vibrant streets deserted.

It was a night like any other. I was walking my beat: a 26-year-old patrolman on his own in the big city during the lonely hours. The period between last call and dawn when it's just you, the pavement, and an odd diffident rat.

It was a crisp fall night. A burst of rain had coated the neighborhood with a slick, reflective sheen. The flickering neon lights from the shuttered bars and liquor stores brushed the sidewalks in a somnolent wash of color.

I knew the territory intimately–from North Avenue to McMechen Street, Linden Avenue to McCulloh Street. Each and every business owner and neighborhood character. All the sweet old ladies and their rambunctious grandkids. The good and the bad, the troublemakers and wise men of this almost exclusively African-American community.

Back in the 1950s, like much of the America, Baltimore was segregated. But the sector I worked was like none other. It was Baltimore's Harlem, and by extension, a great place to work.

'The Avenue' was home to one of the most glamorous entertainment districts I've ever seen. Clubs which hosted some of the greatest musicians of all time, Duke Ellington, Cab Calloway, and of course Baltimore-born Billie Holliday. On Friday or Saturday night the sounds of frenetic saxophone riffs and syncopated rhythms wafted out a line of seemingly endless bars. The street glowed with a sultry electricity I can still feel to this day.

It was an exciting place to work. The type of cosmopolitan atmosphere I don't think exists anymore. And just like the neighborhood, policing then was a different sort of job too.

That s because as already stated, I walked everywhere. I hit the streets without a radio, backup, or a walkie-talkie, just me and my nightstick. I wasn t driving around in technology-laden patrol car. I didn't have GEO location devices or sophisticated computer databases with criminal histories at my disposal. I just had my body and my wits. And a mental picture, as I said before, of the neighborhood in which I served. It was, simply put, a radically different way to police compared to today.

I mean you had to be creative. You couldn t react to a situation with overwhelming force. You couldn't get on the radio and call for backup. You had to collaborate. You had to work with the people you policed. The community was your partner. In other words, you had to form alliances, make friends, and influence people and most importantly, earn their trust.

It wasn t easy, but it was effective.

I bring up this part of my career to make a point. As I witness the disintegration of policing today, I think about my old beat. I think about how different the job was back then, and what I learned walking the beat. How it continues to influence the way I think about policing today.

Too often the debate over effective law enforcement focuses on technology or tactics, body cameras or stun guns, flex cuffs or new patrol cars. We tout things like COMSTAT, a system of monitoring crime statistics that has become the lynchpin of contemporary policing. I watched our current Baltimore police commissioner Kevin Davis tout the efficacy of the so-called 'War Room,' a city-wide surveillance complex he created to address a spike in homicides shortly after the death of Freddie Gray and the ensuing unrest in Baltimore. All these things are nice and look great on TV. But they ignore the most complex and difficult aspect of the job, dealing with people.

That's why walking the beat is better than all technological prowess in the world. Being on foot forces you to confront the community you police in person, among them, and in some sense with them. Not as an impassive arm of the law, but as a somewhat vulnerable human being. Not as a tactical squad stuffed into a rental car on the prowl, but a humble cop ferried about on his own two feet. It's a unique vantage point from which you encounter the people you serve and learn from them.

You became acquainted with store owners and vagrants, young mothers and their sometimes unruly teenagers. The neighborhood's deacons and pastors, the church ladies and the gamblers. Random interactions with people which established ties between you and the community you serve.

You learn the intimate details of their lives: names, birthdays, their triumphs and failures. You comprehend quite quickly how a community is similar to a living breathing human body. A complex and intertwined set of relationships that have more to do with how, why and where crimes occur than all the stats and figures that a COMSTAT board can render.

Some people call this community policing, but if you ask me, there is no such thing. You simply can't police without the community. So I'll give it a different name, a nomenclature I'm making up, but I think is suitable: relational policing. That is, working to enforce the law through a series of substantive relationships with the people. A method of law enforcement that begins with your knowledge of and ties to the people you work for, not statistics and data points.

Perhaps it's just a riff on Sir Robert Peel's principles of policing. A contemporary take on his maxim that you must police with the consent of the community. Because there's no other way to execute effective law enforcement other than to be immersed in the community itself. You have walk among the people so to speak and earn their trust. And you have to be willing to address communal problems, not just as an officer of the law, but as a human being who understands how and why they occur.

So when the call box lit up that evening I would always think first, was it someone I knew? Was a business I had visited that day now the site of a burglary in progress? Was a young mother I chatted with concerned about her children out past curfew?

Just a bit of background. So-called police call boxes were ubiquitous in the 1950s. They were six feet high mounted on a red pole with a beacon affixed to the top. When a call box lit up, that meant someone was in trouble. It is a process similar to radio dispatch, but also different. That's because as I noted earlier in this chapter, the call box was stationary. A permanent fixture rooted in a sidewalk. It was an impassive totem that defined what I could, and couldn't do.

Call boxes were our only lifeline to backup. If you made an arrest, you had to corral the suspect to the call box. If you needed assistance with an unruly crowd, you had to find a call box to call for help. Otherwise, you'd take a long walk with that same person or persons in handcuffs to district headquarters. A dicey bit of maneuvering for a cop by himself.

I mean imagine you just arrested someone four blocks from a call box. And imagine you had to walk that suspect, cooperative or not, four blocks past the row homes and convenience stores, the churches and the recreation centers as everyone watched. If the citizenry didn't trust you, how far do you think you'd make it? And if they didn't believe you were an honest cop, how many times could you pull it off?

Which is why I always approached a call box with trepidation. Opening the box, picking up the receiver was like stepping into the realm of the unknown. A reach into the murky world of circumstance and chance best described by a simple word that characterizes all the underlying disquiet and doubt that sits in the back of the mind of every officer: uncertainty.

What I mean is, back then and even to some degree today, when you go to work as a cop in a complicated city like Baltimore you operate in a constant state of flux. You never know what aspect of human behavior, what horrifying crime, and what small and petty argument between neighborhoods will suddenly become your responsibility. And even worse, you have no idea when human temperament and bad decision making will lead to chaos, violence, and even murder.

It is, in a sense, a spectrum of responsibility that has no limits or fixed boundaries, and when you put on the uniform, you are duty bound to respond to it, and to a certain extent fix it.

It's a different psychology of work than an office job (and I don't mean any disrespect to people who work in offices, I have a variety of relatives from successful lawyer to engineer to financial advisors who excel at their jobs). Working at a desk ensconced inside a cubicle has some structure and surety. Meetings are planned weeks in advance; tasks are laid out in a logical and orderly chronology.

But as a cop in a city like in Baltimore, your office is the streets of a major city. The place you show up for work is often a drug-infested corner in the poorest neighborhood of city all but abandoned by the political establishment. And I think the most unsettling aspect of my job; you have to live with the transformative power of uncertainty, one minute strolling down a street with your nightstick bored and distracted, the next up to your neck in a situation infused with mortal danger and conflict.

The bottom line is when you're a 26-year old cop, and you pick the phone inside the call box, you have no idea what's going to happen next. Your entire being, at that point, is caught up in the throes of uncertainty. An experience that triggers a multitude of contradictory physiological responses: fear, adrenaline, laser focus and even doubt. Nothing about the next ten or twenty minutes may or will be routine. Simply put, you're walking straight into the unknown with little concrete knowledge of what type of scenario awaits.

And that's the dilemma I faced at 2 AM in the morning standing next to the call box on Pennsylvania Ave. The dispatcher was terse. Just an address, and the possibility of a domestic disturbance. That was it. No witness contacts. No cautionary instructions or tactical information. Nothing more than a location and a brief, cursory description.

So with adrenaline pumping in my veins and a myriad of questions swimming in my mind, I started to run towards the scene. It was just four blocks from the call box, so it didn't take me long to get there. Just enough time to recall the one lingering detail from dispatch that heightened the uncertainty quotient, and demonstrates why there is no such thing as a routine call in policing. The apartment was on the second floor.

Baltimore, as you may or may not know, is not a city comprised of skyscrapers and high-rise apartment buildings. It didn't sprout towering office complexes and skyward condos like New York, for example. Instead, the city's housing stock consists of thousands of row homes: modest two-story dwellings that line the city's byways like an ad-hoc assembly line.

Some of the row homes in the neighborhood where I worked were a bit bigger. Four-story structures that housed multiple families, each occupying a living space on a single floor, dividing the building into three or four units. These dwellings were prevalent on the city's East and West sides. Massive homes converted into apartment buildings save one small detail: they were pitch black at night. No brightly lit lobby or well-marked point of egress. Just narrow, dark stairways that connect one landing to the next.

And thats what I confronted when I entered the building: darkness. A nearly pitch black set of stairs leading up to an encounter with the unknown. A path so bereft of light I could barely figure out which way was up. Fortunately, I did carry a flashlight. So I turned it on and began what I'll call the long climb.

As I've already explained, there's a certain amount terror, yes terror that comes with the job of being a cop. As they say, we run towards danger, not away from it. It's an axiom that sounds pretty straightforward, but it's not. That's because the situations you're running towards are often practically unpredictable and dangerously unwieldy.

Its one thing to be part of a cadre of officers arriving on the scene of bank robbery, or a group of cops honing in at the aftermath shooting. Both those scenes are equally if not more dangerous than what I was confronting. In fact, for all I knew at the end of the stairs was a missing cat and an apoplectic child.

But something about being alone, about walking up the steps not knowing, makes policing a singular experience. Entering an unfamiliar apartment building at an hour when the world is asleep, and you've been working the night shift for months. The initiation into the darkness that starts the mind spinning and puts your instinctual reflexes on high alert that cannot compare to any other experience I've ever had. In some sense, those fifteen or so steps up the stairs could have been my last. A brief interlude or solitude punctuated by a spasm of violence.

I'm not trying to be melodramatic or engender fake sympathy for cops. Fear and risk is simply part of the job. If you signed up to be a cop, you better expect it. What I'm trying to communicate is the psychology of being there, at that moment. How on any given day you could suddenly find yourself in a situation alone in the murky world of darkness running up an unfamiliar set of stairs. A climb that could well be the place where you spend the last moments of your life.

Of course, at the time I was barreling up those same stairs I wasn't contemplating the philosophy of police work, I was working off adrenaline, a little bit of training, and a whole lot of the bravado that prompts young men to run into the darkness ... not away from it.

When I mounted the second-floor landing, I heard two distinct voices, one raised, the other apparently distraught. I could hear movement behind the door. And worst of all, panic in what sounded like a female's protestations, and anger in the male's response. I didn't need to see through the walls to confirm it was, in fact, a domestic.

The door was locked, so I knocked. I heard footsteps and the muffled sounds of an argument. It was heated but muted. Soon the door cracked open just a bit. A small sliver of light obscured my view of what was inside.

A child appeared, a young girl who looked up at me with calm eyes. She seemed, in her gestures and casual apprehension of me accustomed to disorder, almost oblivious to what was occurring inside her home.

She said nothing while opening the door a little wider then quietly disappearing into the darkness of the abode.

So I slipped inside. To my left, I could hear the voices of two adults, a man, and woman. The girl disappeared. I headed towards conflict, what else could I do? My best hope was the presence of a police officer would calm whatever conflict was stoking tensions inside.

That of course, was a naive presumption. A strategy necessitated by the reality of being the lone man on the block. Like I've already mentioned, I didn t have access to overwhelming force or even readily accessible backup. And even if I did, it wouldn t be the paramilitary stuff you see today. Maybe, if I were lucky, I could summon the guy walking the beat in the next sector.

Maybe.

Suddenly, the woman screamed. I bolted towards the kitchen. She was falling back on her heels, tumbling out of the doorway and onto the living room floor. The young girl shrieked. Just a few steps from the commotion, a man emerged, holding a knife.

He was a formidable physical presence. At least over six feet tall and I guessed roughly two hundred plus pounds. He had the bulging forearms of a blue-collar laborer. A man who I figured worked with steel, or pig iron, or some other industrial product long since abandoned. Bottom line, he outweighed me, and more than likely could take me in hand to hand combat.

He paused for a moment to size me up. His eyes were darting back and forth from his wife to me. A cop who at that point had not even had the time to draw his gun. So we just both stood there for one of those eternal moments. Both of us waiting for someone to make a move. That split second of indecisiveness that often determines who lives and dies.

Of course, if I were trained in contemporary tactics, my gun would already have been pointed at him. I would have been aiming for center mass, screaming at him to drop the knife. The confrontation would have escalated, and who knows what would've happened next. Tragedy maybe, death for one us, the bottom line: not much good.

Maybe thats what I was thinking and why I hesitated to take my gun out of my holster. I hadn't yet had the experience I recounted in my first book, the pain, and horror of shooting and killing a hold-up man in West Baltimore. So the consequences of making a life or death decision weren't something I completely understood. But I think I knew enough at that moment that it's not the outcome I wanted.

But I also believe my split second of hesitation had something to do with the way I had learned to police. As I already explained, walking the beat engenders a different mentality. You interact with people; you don t drive past them. Ambling about on your two feet is a great equalizer. And the random interactions with the public it precipitates changes the psychology of being a cop. Familiarity does decidedly not breed contempt. In fact quite the opposite, it engenders empathy and interconnectedness.

So I stood still, sizing up this man who had emerged from the kitchen seemingly enraged. I wanted to see him first before I acted. I needed a glimpse of his face. To get a sense of his state of mind, what he intended to do.

Yes, it was a risky strategy. I guess you could say a man brandishing a knife bathed in sweat is hardly an enigma. What else did I need to know?

But for whatever reason, I wasn't ready to shoot him.

I'm not trivializing the risk I was facing. I was ten feet away from him. It would have taken two seconds from him to stride across the living room and cut my gut open. He was not a benign threat.

But he also had stood completely still since our initial encounter. I think he was stunned that a cop was standing in his living room. Maybe he was just as unsure of what to do next as I was.

Of course, domestics are one of the most dangerous situations a cop faces, even more perilous than car stops.

I've witnessed first hand how the volatility of family dynamics can push a man to the precipice of violence and then over it. Often, the presence of a police officer only makes the abuser angrier, and more likely to act out. That's one of the reasons I didn't immediately escalate; I wanted him to know there were other options.

So that was it. A man in a seemingly desperate and violent state, and a young beat cop standing inside a strange apartment staring at the sharp blade of a wavering kitchen knife. Five minutes earlier, I'd been thinking about what I was going to eat for breakfast at the end of my shift. Now I was thrust into a conflict demanding split-second life or death decisions.

Remember what I said about uncertainty? How about simple and immutable terror? Confronting an angry husband trapped inside a cramped apartment wielding a kitchen knife large enough to eviscerate a side of beef. My night shift of aimless boredom transformed into a rendezvous with deadly violence in a matter of seconds.

But as we stood there, eyes locked on each other, waiting for someone to make a move something happened: a wholly unexpected development that changed the tenor of the encounter in a matter of moments. An unexpected twist in the story inextricably linked to walking the beat, how it changes policing, how it made me a better cop. I recognized him.

"Sam," I said, making a connection between him and another man I knew well: his cousin Mike.

Mike was one of those communal characters, ambitious, opinionated, and talkative. A man who knew the neighborhood, its troubles and underlying conflicts intimately.

Just a few days ago, I bumped into Mike outside to district headquarters. Standing next to him was his cousin, Sam, the same man holding a knife. A member of the community whose life depended upon the decisions I would make in the next sixty seconds.

Mike introduced me to Sam. Later he told me Sam was having problems at work. He was a welder, and business was slow. His employer had cut his hours, and he was afraid he would lose his job. But at that moment I hoped the simple fact I knew him would help defuse the increasingly dangerous situation.

"Mike's cousin, right?" I asked.

He stood and stared at me for a moment. He was, it seemed, stunned. Perhaps he didn't remember meeting me. Maybe he just wasn't paying attention. Sometimes the uniform blurs distinctions; sometimes cops just look alike.

But I had his attention. For a brief moment, he seemed to let down his guard. The knife slowly dropping to his side.

"Mike told me, he explained your trouble at work," I offered. "I was talking to him the other day. Whatever happens, it's not worth it. It's just not."

Sam flinched. He looked down at the knife, then back at me. He didn't utter a word. He just stood there, I guess contemplating what I'd said. Or maybe he was trying to process the fact that a cop standing in his living room knew something about him.

"Sam, put down the knife," I said as calmly as I could. "If you use it, you can't take it back. It's not going to make anything better," I added. "Things will work out if you just put down the knife."

He looked at me, the sort of unwieldy glare of a man who can't fully corral his emotions. For what seemed like an eternity, he stood in place. His arms slackened, his grip on the knife eased. His head slowly bent as his eyes cast towards the floor and his face slackened.

Then, the knife dropped from his hand onto the floor. The woman, I assumed was his wife began to sob. At the time I didn't realize how tense I was too. I could feel my body unwind. My hand hovering above my gun relax. I took a deep breath.

"Sam, I'm going to pick up the knife, don't move."

And he didn't. In fact, he even retreated a bit. A single backward step into the kitchen.

I walked slowly across the living room and gently cradled the knife in the palm of my hand. Sam just watched. His face contorted with pain. A human being seemingly caught in the inexorable downward spiral of the economic stagnation which two decades later would take hold of the city and not let go. The inevitable fiscal decline that would turn Baltimore upside down, and transform the lowered expectations of people like Sam into a plague of irrepressible violence.

But at that moment, all those ills were entangled in the misfortune of one man. A man who moments before posed a mortal threat. And now he seemed on the verge of collapse into a violent emotional state of misguided anger and inexpressible rage. He was lost, and it was my job to guide him and his family to safety.

For a few seconds, again, we both stood there and said nothing. Two men equally terrified and unsure of what would happen next. Both of us wanting the conflict to end. Just two human beings not exactly sure what to do next.

But I faced another dilemma too. If I did resolve the situation peacefully, what should I do with Sam? Technically threatening someone with a knife was at the very least a second-degree assault and perhaps warranted an even more serious charge. I couldn't just walk out the apartment and leave his wife and child unprotected.

Sam appeared to have calmed a bit. I asked him to wait in the kitchen. I then escorted his wife to a bedroom where I questioned her about what happened. It was risky, leaving Sam by himself. He could easily pick up the knife and thrust it into my chest. But I hoped our connection instilled enough trust that he would remain put as promised.

In the bedroom, his wife recounted what happened before my arrival.

"It's the job," she said. "He didn't touch me, but I'm scared. I'm scared, for both of us. He didn t mean me no harm, no harm at all," she added.

It was not an unusual story from a spouse. She too was cognizant of the dilemma both she and Sam faced. Jail could mean more hardship and uncertainty. Imprisonment perhaps the final blow against his already tenuous hold on work.

But his continued presence in the apartment and lack of intervention by me could also result in more conflict, and even danger. Like I said before, domestics are often the most complicated and dicey cases a cop confronts, and there's usually no good outcome or simple solution to keep everyone both safe and happy. After all, he brandished a knife and threatened both his wife and me.

Still, the fact that he didn't touch her was helpful, while not completely exonerating. The ambiguity of the situation raised an even uglier aspect of the daunting uncertainty that rules the lives of cops.

Let's say I look the other way. My sympathy for the family and Sam s work predicament prompts me to let him go.

Two days later, Sam is laid off. And a week later, he erupts in a fury and kills his wife. Whose fault is it? Who are the politicians and the public going to blame?

Well not Sam, even though he committed the crime. Not the economic system which disrupts the lives of men like Sam and puts them out of work.

They'll blame me. Because It happened on my watch, and because I was the officer on the scene. Whatever occurs, whatever choices Sam makes after our encounter is my responsibility. It might not be fair, hell it might not even be rational, but that's the way it is.

So after I talked to his wife, I asked Sam if we could take a walk. I wanted to get him out of the apartment without a commotion. "Lets take a walk," I suggested. "You need to cool off."

And for some reason, he trusted me enough to comply.

So we walked. Past the liquor stores and the bars, the corner groceries and the storefront churches. We talked. About his aspirations for the children and his concerns about his work. About his growing anxiety that he would soon be unable to support his family. The anger and frustration he felt about the world could not provide enough substantive opportunity for an honest man willing to work hard.

When we arrived at district headquarters, I told Sam I had to charge him with second-degree assault. It was a minor crime, the least serious offense given the circumstances. I also promised I would speak to the judge to persuade him to release Sam on his own recognizance.

Sam wasn't happy. He pleaded with me to look the other way. But I told him I had to charge him with something because he threatened both myself and his wife with a knife. I also said I would stand by him during the court proceedings. I promised I would urge the judge to let him go without bail. I would vouch for him as much as I could.

Fortunately, he went along with the plan. I arrested him without any trouble. He was home by morning because his case was adjudicated at the district headquarters where the proceedings were fast, efficient, and over within hours.

I never talked to Sam again. Prosecutors ended up dropping the charges. His cousin told me he managed to keep the job, and his wife. I don't know what eventually happened to the man, but I learned a lesson that I think holds true even more today than it did then.

With an emphasis on numbers, technology, aggressiveness, and overwhelming force policing has become a process of dehumanization for both the cops who do it and the people they serve. We've lost our connections to those same people along the way, and as a result, we've changed the job so fundamentally sometimes I barely recognize it.

Walking the beat, although arduous and often risky, made my job easier. That's because I knew people I policed in ways both intimate and useful. A meaningful set of relationships from which to begin the often vexing and unpleasant job of enforcing the law.

It was a connection that would serve me well and occasionally saved me. A way of practicing policing that informed every aspect of my career with a simple resonant truth: you can't police a community if you don't know it.

But more importantly, I also learned the complexity of single human being is impossible to comprehend from behind a windshield. That the summary and superficial judgments we make sitting in headquarters studying data teach us little about the very human process of crime. That to police a community, you must immerse yourself in it.

Perhaps walking the beat instead of cruising around in a patrol car is analogous to abandoning Facebook or social media for face-to-face interaction. Or taking a college course online versus learning by sitting in a classroom. There is something inimical about interacting in the flesh. It mediates the void that otherwise consumes us. When we emerge from the digital ether and enter the world or things, our thinking becomes more nuanced, empathetic, and intrinsically human.

That same type of transformation occurs when a cop walks the beat. Officer and citizen inhabit the same space and in sense share a communal common ground. Crime becomes not an isolated data point but a continuum of behavior and discernable patterns that are both easier to comprehend and solve. The task of keeping the peace turns into a collective process built upon the foundation of interdependency and personal relations.

That was what I learned walking the beat. A lesson I think is applicable today. In fact, more than ever I believe much of what ails the relationship between police and community is the space between us. An occupational divide which subsumes our ability to work together. To be partners, not adversaries connected by the mutual goal of building better communities.

CHAPTER THREE:
POISON OF THE MIND

Would a man intentionally poison himself?

Would he knowingly drink a toxic substance that would literally turn his esophagus and stomach lining into mush? Is it possible that a living human being–say he was a bit delusional–choose a slow, painful and excruciating death? And what does it say about human nature if indeed a person would intentionally inflict self-harm for reasons that are completely inexplicable?

What if it was a cop who did it? A Baltimore police detective who drank a poisonous substance, either knowingly or unwittingly? A young man who became so sick he ended up in a coma. And whose friends and relatives believed he might have been the victim of foul play, even though there was almost no evidence to prove it?

It's a question I've asked myself on occasion when I think about a strange case that involved the death of a police officer nearly 50 years ago which remains a mystery. An investigation that in many ways poses vexing questions not just about crime, but people. An unsolved case involving the sudden death of an otherwise healthy police detective. A man who slipped into a coma and died in the ICU of Union Memorial hospital without warning or provocation. And another weird chapter in the so-called land of the unsolved that still haunts me due to the cases twisted ambiguities and illusory evidence.

As I discussed throughout both my books, there are cases that remain unsolved because we don't do our job; murders that could be closed with a little hard work and more effective investigation. But then there are some suspicious deaths which fall into a different category altogether. A no mans land, so to speak, where all the wisdom, investigative prowess, and solid police work dont make a difference. Deaths that might be murders, suicides, accidents, or simply put, mysteries. And the story I am about to tell falls into that category: a mystery.

That doesn't mean I care less or don't take the blame myself for not closing them. The simple fact is when I can't solve a case it means that someone got away with a crime. It doesn't matter whether it's a straightforward shooting or more convoluted act of odd circumstance and unrepentant malice.

But even worse or I suppose more painful for a wizened old detective are cases so twisted and bizarre that I never really figure out the truth. Odd circumstances and inexplicable events which become markers of not just personal failure, but symbols of the pervasive murkiness which often convolutes the way people die in a city so unrepentantly violent.

Which is why I still think about the case that stumped me nearly 50 years ago. It involved a cop, poison, and more misdirection and errant clues than I've dealt with in my entire career. A mysterious death long forgotten I still think about to this day. A story about the horrifying end of one man's life that starts with the most profound question a police officer confronts: what are we capable of?

It is a query predicated in part upon the unknown capacities of the mind. An attempt to comprehend the actual human potential for both self-destructiveness and self- harm. And in doing so, elicit all the ambiguities hidden in the vast and mysterious expanses of the human psyche.

So with that thought, I will reiterate the question I asked at the beginning of the chapter. Would a man knowingly drink a toxic substance? Could he gulp down a toxic chemical with full knowledge it might kill him?

Or would someone else, devious and venal slowly poison a man to death? Would a human being intentionally and torturously harm another to the point they lapse into a coma and waste away in a hospital bed?

Or is there an entirely different scenario we just couldn't and don't want to contemplate?

Those were just a few of the troubling questions I faced in summer of 1973 when I received one of the strangest phone calls in my career. I was a homicide supervisor and occasional internal affairs investigator, the first to ever serve in the Baltimore police department.

Back then, that particular line of work was a pretty lonely. We didn't have staff, just me. And we were just as unpopular with the rank and file as we were today, except there wasn't a department filled with dozens of investigators to diffuse the blowback. I took the heat myself, and it wasn't pretty.

If you think the blue line is thick now back then it was like a fortress. Remember, the idea of an internal affairs department or cops investigating cops was new, at least in Baltimore. It was simply something we just didn't do, intentionally put a cop in jail. And since I was technically the first, I was treated with even more suspicion and contempt than an internal affairs detective is today

A few years earlier as I chronicled in *You Can t Stop Murder*, I'd lead a major investigation of police involved in an illegal gambling operation at a hotel on Pennsylvania Avenue in West Baltimore. It was a massive case replete with surveillance footage and tons of physical evidence in the form of betting slips, eyewitnesses, and even ledgers. But somewhere along the way, my search and seizure warrant went missing. A critical piece of paper that disappeared during the initial raid and then mysteriously reappeared in the newsroom of *The Baltimore Sun* during the trial.

So even with cops caught on film both entering and leaving the site of a massive gambling operation along with credible testimony from witnesses who worked for it, only two convictions resulted from one of the biggest police sting operations in the history of the department. I think it did more damage to my reputation among my fellow cops than it did to discourage them from taking part in illicit gambling.

But the case I m about to recount wasn t about crooked cops or a numbers racket. It's actually about the death of detective under suspicious circumstances. A man who wasted away in Union Memorial hospital for no apparent reason until we found one. And when we did, it was as baffling and unsettling as some of the most inexplicable murders I ever investigated.

As I said, the case started with a phone call to homicide. A supervisor reporting to us that one of his police detectives was in a coma in the intensive care unit. He was concerned the officer was a victim of foul play. Even worse, he told us the doctors didn t think the young man was going to survive. And they didn t know why he was dying. "He was real sick before he was admitted, throwing up, dizzy, and confused," the supervisor told me. "His friend said he had a couple of beers, and that's when he started feeling sick."

"And then he just passed out."

I've already noted, it was an odd call. I'm accustomed to responding to horrifying crimes, violence and shootings, stabbings and beatings. But an officer on his deathbed because he drank a couple of beers? It was more than weird; it didn t make any sense.

What, I wondered, could put a young detective in the hospital without any obvious explanation? What type of affliction could he have contracted that doctors could not yet diagnose?

Could he be one of many cops I've encountered in my career that succumbed to the temptations of drug abuse and had simply drunk himself to near death? Had he come down with some mysterious and otherwise identifiable disease? And the most terrifying prospect of all;

was his affliction something truly mysterious beyond our immediate grasp? Worse yet, the man who could most likely tell me was unconscious, fighting for his life in the ICU.

So we as drove to the hospital, my mind was churning. Its my own peculiar process of mental preparation. Mulling over what I knew searching for possible lines of investigation that could explain the facts.

My brain would work furiously to conjure critical questions and plausible answers. Why was an otherwise (as far I knew) healthy cop lying unconscious in a hospital bed? What transformed a relatively young man into a comatose vegetable? What were the possible scenarios that could explain how a presumably disease-free detective would wind up on his deathbed?

When we arrived at Union Memorial, the victim had a contingent of relatives staked outside the ICU unit. Among them, several cousins, a brother, and his wife. We spoke briefly to the doctor. He told us the prognosis was grim. He didn't think the detective would regain consciousness. And the physician speculated, given his symptoms, that he might have somehow imbibed poison. He didn't know what kind of poison, but the fact that an otherwise healthy man was dying in the ICU without any other signs of disease, poison seemed to be the only logical explanation.

So now we had quite a dilemma. The kind of case that makes the run of the mill violent homicide look simple.

Shooting someone in the head is the preferred method of murder in Baltimore. It's an act that usually produces a significant amount of physical evidence. But finding the means and opportunity to deliver poison to an unwitting man, to pick out a notably lethal chemical and administer it in doses that would ultimately kill him?

That was the work of a different kind of killer: a methodical and determined sociopath. Someone willing to go to great and unusual lengths to kill, and even more extreme measures to conceal their role in it. But that scenario seemed unlikely given the city's penchant for a more personalized form of vengeance.

Baltimore, also known as Mobtown, is the land of point and shoot murder. When people want to kill, they are hardly shy about it. Blunt force trauma, stabbings, the random shot to the head. That's how the killers of Baltimore get it done, and that's what I was accustomed to investigating.

But the devious and seemingly discrete task of stealthily filling someone's body with a lethal poison is quite a different method of killing. It takes intricate planning, a devious mind and lots of strategic thinking. It is a crime requiring acute duplicity.

Still, I didn't know if the spoisoning was intentional or accidental. In fact, I didn't even have a clue as to exactly what was killing him. The doctors at Union Memorial had flushed his kidneys to save his life. Consequently, there was little left of whatever was prompting his organs to shut down like overworked pistons in a malfunctioning combustion engine.

Making matters worse were rumors that were spreading throughout the department like wildfire. Officers who believed the detective had been working vice on the block and had dug up some dirt on his superiors. It wasn't clear what kind of dirt, but the story was he was fed a spiked drink nightly to keep him quiet. A prolonged murder plot that after two weeks of toxic cocktails did him in.

I didn't have any evidence the tale was true. All I knew was that a young man was dying, and we didn't know why.

So we focused on his relatives in search of clues. His daughter was distraught and inconsolable. So was his wife. Both weren't in good enough psychological shape to talk to us at the hospital.

But as we gathered names and addresses of the relatives and assorted friends gathered at his bedside, one of his fellow officers asked if he could speak with me privately. So we stepped outside the detective s crowded hospital room.

"A few days before he got sick he was telling everybody there was a $50,000 contract on his life," the detective whispered in the hallway. "When he got here just before he passed out he was still talking about it."

"Do you have any information as to who that might be?"

"No sir," he responded. "It was the first I d heard of it."

It was a whopper of a clue. A critical piece of information that momentarily turned the case of a mysterious illness into a homicide investigation. In a sense, it made the probe even more daunting and critical. The possibility of a contract on a cop s life raised the stakes. So I called his supervisor to obtain more details.

"Yeah, he said he was getting death threats and that one of his perps was out to get him," his supervisor told us. "It seemed weird, but he kept telling us someone wanted him dead."

"Is that true?" I asked.

"No way," the supervisor replied. "Not as far as I know. Truthfully," he added, "I can't think of another detective who worked more routine cases and would be less likely to be in trouble. I mean he staked out a few illegal lotteries and made some minor arrests, nothing that would put him in that sort of bind."

In fact, I spoke with another supervisor who had intimate knowledge of his case work. He told me the detective rarely worked narcotics, which is a dangerous beat that often entails interacting with violent suspects. Instead, his primary assignment had been low-level investigations of illegal gambling. A light caseload marked by small-time busts. Most important, his supervisors assured me his arrest record didn t involve enough high-level suspects to warrant threats. In other words, he was more than likely telling tall tales.

Maybe.

And so I was faced with new a dilemma, a quandary that returned me to my initial query about the vagaries of human nature. Why would someone fabricate something as serious as death threats?

Believe me, I have some experience with existential threats. Years ago a murder suspect threatened to kill me in open court. There was an officer stationed outside my house for weeks. My family was terrified. My eldest daughter traumatized. So it's not something I take lightly. But in this case, I couldn't find any evidence it was true. And if he was making this up, what was his motive and how far was he willing to go to turn fiction into fact? All these questions became more critical when we sat down with his wife.

Initially, she simply recounted the painful details of the progression of her husband's apparent illness. How he had drunk a few beers, then slumped down the couch. How he couldn t stand up and became dizzy and disoriented. How he vomited and then complained of severe stomach pains. How she panicked and called one of his friends to take him to the hospital.

And then she said something that piqued my curiosity.

"He was fine," she told me, "until he went out and started working on the car."

"Car, where?"

"In the garage."

"And when he was finished you said he starting getting sick?" I asked.

"Yes," she replied. "He was dizzy and said his stomach was hurting. He could barely stand, that s why we took him to the hospital."

"Do you know what he was doing with the car, repair work or something?"

"I don't. I heard the trunk open and close, that's it."

"And was that the last thing he had done before he got sick?"

"Yeah," she said. "After that, he started throwing up."

It wasn t a major clue, but it was something. It gave me a starting point. A time when he was functional, and a time when he was not.

When she finished, we asked her if we could take a look at the car. She gave us the keys, and we headed towards the spot where the young and perhaps troubled detective spent his last healthy minutes on earth.

The first thing we did was open the trunk. It was our initial and up until then only lead. Perhaps something inside would explain the bizarre sequence of events that up until now seemed inexplicable. Something that could shed a little light on what occurred before he was hospitalized. And thankfully when we I turned the key and opened the hatch of his 1971 Chevy Impala, we encountered the first clue as to what might have transformed a healthy man into a corpse in a matter of hours.

Buried under a pile of rags was a partially open bottle of antifreeze. It was half full. The cap was loose, and some of the fluid had seeped into a rag stuffed into the nozzle.

But what did it mean? Well, maybe nothing. A poorly stored bottle of antifreeze is hardly a smoking gun. Maybe the detective was just topping off his radiator as he sipped a beer. A perfectly normal American ritual.

But there was a pattern in the set of coincidences culminating in the leaking container of solvent buried in the trunk. A Baltimore Police detective was dying for no apparent reason from a sudden onset of mortal illness that no one could explain. And the doctor seemed confident that poison was the cause. And now I was staring at a half empty bottle of antifreeze.

Of course, at that point, I didn't have any proof that he had antifreeze in his system. But after picking up that bottle and examining it, the so-called bells of interconnectedness started to ring in my head. Meaning once distinctive and seemingly unrelated facts began to link together to form a plausible theory.

To advance the hunch that was starting to gel in mind, I examined the radiator itself. Was it empty? Or was it full? Had he recently topped it off or was it instead in need of fluid?

We measured and found it was roughly three-quarters full. Not a solid clue, but another piece of evidence suggesting the missing fluid hadn't necessarily ended up inside a radiator. Logic dictates that if he had just opened up a bottle of radiator fluid, it would end up in the tank. Not irrefutable evidence, a partially empty radiator and a half full bottle of fluid, but useful.

Next, we checked back with the doctor. His prognosis: death was imminent. So I asked, could he check the detective for traces of the active ingredient in radiator fluid: ethylene glycol.

"No, I can't do that because as I told you we flushed his kidneys," he said. "We'll have to wait until the autopsy toxicology."

So, like many cases, we had a few clues and a hunch, but nothing conclusive. The less than full bottle of antifreeze could indicate that he drank it. But maybe he simply poured it down a drain. A half empty radiator certainly could bolster the theory the fluid ended up somewhere other than where it belonged. But all of the clues were ambiguous. Not a single fact pointed towards a definitive theory. Just circumstantial evidence bolstered by a vague set of motives.

So like many cops, I turned to my own personal methodology to help. One of several philosophies of investigation I use to piece together ambiguous facts and conflicting evidence into a cohesive set of assumptions. In this case, the postulate known as Occam's Razor.

Occam's Razor is a basic rule of logic formulated by William of Occam; a 12th-century theologian and scholar. His concept was simple: the least complicated solution to a problem, the approach with the smallest set of variables, is usually correct.

It is an axiom generally applied to scientific experimentation. But a methodology I found useful for organizing a set of facts gathered during a criminal investigation. Especially when evidence appeared inherently illogical and contradictory.

Of course, I also always kept in mind the converse to Occam's razor: the law of entropy. Also known as the second law of thermodynamics, it means that nature tends towards disorder. That is, things eventually fall apart. Or, inevitably, the most efficacious and seemingly orderly investigation can descend into dead ends and irreconcilable leads in a matter of minutes.

Both modes of analysis seemed to be relevant in this case. Because when the doctor told me the detective had, in fact, died, all I had to go on was a half-empty bottle of radiator fluid and a half-baked theory about a man who might have drunk it.

So let's apply Occam's razor to the evidence at hand. Let's test it against two distinctly different scenarios that were both plausible based on the evidence.

Scenario One: The detective drank radiator fluid to poison himself intentionally. Scenario One involves a cop who potentially suffers from either a delusion of grandeur or insurmountable insecurity. That same cop tries to convince his peers of imminent peril. However, his story gains little traction, according to his supervisors. So he decides to inflict just enough self-harm to make the case. His method: poison.

Maybe he does some research and reads about the effect radiator fluid has on the body. Perhaps he knows the active ingredient can cause some dramatic symptoms, including vomiting, dizziness, and headaches. And maybe he learns that there's an antidote for it, namely consuming lots of alcohol.

And so, with a little bit of knowledge and a single purchase of relatively inexpensive household material he's secured a safe way to stage a dramatic event to prove his police work is just as dangerous as he asserts.

It's a simple albeit troubling explanation based on the evidence at hand: he had access to the poison, he had the motivation and the opportunity.

Now let's examine scenario two: someone else we had yet to identify, for reasons yet unknown, decided to poison the detective unbeknown to him.

From an evidentiary perspective, there was no indication among the assortment of relatives and colleagues we spoke to anyone was out to get him. In fact, we administered lie detector tests to sixteen people who were either related or close associate just to ascertain if anyone in his immediate circle had a motive or opportunity to administer the poison surreptitiously. Everyone passed.

We also learned he was having problems with his wife, but she had a perfect alibi on the night he got sick. She also passed the lie detector test.

And that particular evening was the first time his daughter and other witnesses told us he had exhibited the symptoms that presaged his demise. Thus, whoever did it, had to be near or around him and have access to whatever he was drinking that evening. They would have to slip the toxic substance into his beer unnoticed. Then that same suspect would have to make sure he drank the poison cocktail. A fatal dose delivered without the knowledge of the detective.

Now I'm not an expert on radiator fluid as a mixer, but it would be pretty difficult, if not impossible, to disguise it in quantities sufficient to kill. Yes, it tastes sweet and is not like drinking gasoline, for example. But it is noticeable enough to be detected in quantities sufficient to kill. You could not dole it out in small doses in order to poison someone slowly. The body flushes it out. If your goal is to kill someone slowly over time it would be much easier to use a stealthier and old school poison like arsenic.

In fact, I checked with several chemists about the possibility a would-be murderer could disguise the taste of ethylene glycol. They told me perhaps in small doses it would be possible to conceal it in a strong alcoholic drink. But the three to four ounces it would take to kill a man, simply not plausible, the stuff was too toxic.

So given Occam's explicit preference for simplicity expressed in Occam's Razor, which explanation make more sense? Which scenario is less complicated and simpler with the fewest number of variables? Exactly, self-administered. And by the way, we checked a discarded beer can we found in the kitchen trash can. No trace of radiator fluid.

Thus I had a plausible working theory based upon the simplest explanation of the evidence at hand. What I like to call a starting point. It's like locating Polaris or the North Star in the sky and reorienting your path by moving towards it. Once you have a good sense of direction, the landscape starts to make sense. It's the most basic and elemental technique of a sound investigation. Find the pieces of the puzzle that fit, assemble a picture however incomplete of what you do and don't know, and then gather more clues.

Of course, this technique of supposition has flaws. Invariably it can fuel speculative thinking and often unverifiable assumptions. And while there's nothing inherently wrong with theorizing, a good investigator tries to remain both flexible and open-minded. It's pretty easy to let a hunch prompt you to ignore or even avoid the contradictory evidence. It's a weakness of the human mind to become overly attached to a personal theory. It's a phenomenon social scientists call confirmation bias: amassing a set of facts to fit your expectations while purposely ignoring any evidence that challenges your assumptions. Still, if you're mindful of not getting too stuck on a single explanation of what happened, painting a speculative picture is an essential tool to effectively figuring a case out.

So I had a dead cop lying on a gurney in Union Memorial with blood so toxic his organs were practically pickled. I didn't have a single shred of evidence to substantiate threats against his life. And his wife told us that just before he became sick, he was futzing around in the garage rummaging through the trunk of his car.

But of course, like many cases, the simplest explanation was also the most daunting.

I didn't have a toxicology report. I didn't have any direct evidence that he had indeed drunk the fluid. And I didn't have any actual witnesses who had seen him drink the alleged suicidal cocktail before his demise.

So I decided to interview his wife again. I wanted to establish a timeline. The idea was to determine the interval between when he was in the garage, and when he started getting sick.

Our talk was productive. She was sharp and attentive, answering each question thoughtfully. She gave us the time when the detective entered the garage, and interval between when he left and began to exhibit symptoms. So with her help we were able to establish a timeline from exactly when he was proximate to the car and when the first symptoms of illness emerged. According to what she told us, it took roughly an hour give or take a few minutes, between his visit to the garage and the onset of illness. A period of time that would provide critical support for my theory that he possibly poisoned himself. It was just the dot I needed to connect a few more.

So after we talked to every possible person and assembled the scant medical evidence, we created a rudimentary timeline of events. We collated it into a working file and then began the task of digging deeper. Another step in the investigative process that also adheres to my philosophy of detective work: search for context.

What do I mean?

Facts don't exist in a vacuum. Meaning there is a world of scientists, technology experts, and others who can help shed light on what you know ... and more importantly, what you don't. And its the search to augment facts with context that can play an important role in successfully completing an investigation.

In this case, we knew how much time elapsed between when he was rummaging in the trunk and when he first became symptomatic. This timeline provided an important clue. We could now compare the scientifically determined lapse between a dose radiator fluid and symptoms and the actual amount of time it took for the detective to take ill after he entered the garage. If the two time periods correlated, we had a better factual basis for assuming he poisoned himself.

Again, it might not provide definitive proof, but the comparison would at the very least broaden our understanding of what might have occurred by providing relevant and meaningful context.

So I wrote to Union Carbide, the manufacture of ethylene glycol, the primary chemical found in antifreeze. I asked them exactly how long would it take for a person who had drunk the amount missing from bottle to exhibit symptoms of toxicity. The company was helpful, they wrote back quickly with a definitive answer.

One hour.

And even more pertinent, a company chemist estimated it would take exactly three hours for organs to begin shutting down. Within three hours, the chemist concluded, the person would lose consciousness, lapse into a coma, and without an antidote, die. The timing was perfect. It matched the progression of the detective's condition almost to the minute. If he had indeed drunk antifreeze, science predicted his transition from asymptomatic to death within minutes.

The next piece of 'context' came from the Union Memorial doctor. He told us about a special test available in Washington DC which could determine if there were residual traces of ethylene glycol in the cells of the body, even if the subject was deceased. So we forwarded tissue sample to the laboratory and again got a hit. He had indeed ingested radiator fluid. However the substance got into his body, the primary ingredient of antifreeze is what ultimately killed him.

Of course the evidence, as strong as it was, couldn't tell us what was going on in his mind. We didn't or couldn't know what the man was thinking. Yes, we had an inkling based on the information gathered from friends and colleagues. They all agreed he was a bit delusional about the risks of his job. But they also told us that it seemed to be a harmless neurosis, nothing more than cop braggadocio, about as common among police as a cold.

So what exactly could I do? Referring back to Occam's Razor I looked for the simplest explanation based upon the evidence. Our detective has a bit of an ego problem. He wants his peers to believe he is a heroic cop constantly flaunting danger. He brags about the risks of the mean streets but hasn't yet encountered a perp that matches his bluster. He tells tall tales of big busts and nefarious crime bosses. But none of his actual exploits match his histrionics.

So to bolster his rep he fabricates mortal threats, recounts stories about how his life is imperiled by a suspect. Maybe a kingpin drug dealer or a homicidal maniac. Or a vengeance seeking numbers man whose operation he took down with a death-defying bust.

But how does he substantiate this fiction? What can he do to make the harrowing tales of both bravery and malice seem real and convincing?

Well, a self-inflicted gunshot wound is messy, and dangerous. And also not easy to stage. Obviously, a beating presents the same problems. Awkward and potentially dangerous. But drinking some poison, that might work. Given the evidence, its not unreasonable to suppose this wanna-be hero drinks some poison to show his friends that he's living the life he purports to.

The toxin would act slowly enough, he believes, so he would have time to drink the antidote before the symptoms overwhelm him. Maybe he even takes a trip to the emergency room to heighten the drama. Or maybe just gets sick enough to prompt the kind of worry and concern that would give his friend and colleagues pause. I mean just minutes before he lost consciousness he was babbling about a $50,000 contract on his life.

But something goes wrong. The self-administered dose overwhelms him. His body can't handle it. And he becomes disoriented and incapacitated before he can take an antidote. The plan goes too well. Death overtakes him before he can save himself. His mind loses clarity too soon. His inflated ego and plan for providential affirmation die together. A mortal confluence of an insecure psyche, lack of ingenuity and bad timing that culminated in death.

Its a terrible tale if true. But it was also the only explanation I had.

I did consult a police psychiatrist about the detective's state of mind before his death. I handed over all the evidence we'd gathered during our investigation. The doctor concurred with my analysis. He concluded that the detective had developed a level of constant paranoia, which may have been the precursor to a more severe mental illness, all precipitated by the pressure he felt to fulfill unrealistic or imaginary work expectations.

Sadly, because I didn't have the concrete evidence to prove my hypothesis, the medical examiner ruled the death undetermined, meaning he couldn't classify it in one of four primary causes of death: homicide, suicide, accident, or natural causes. We were able to tell the family what killed him, but not why.

And frankly, I didn't want to share my theory. How would I explain to his grieving wife her husband intentionally drank antifreeze in a misguided attempt to fashion himself into a hero?

No good way I could think of.

The hard part is I don't know for sure what happened. I'm not privy to the thoughts of a dead man. My hypothesis was all supposition. Theories that don't hold weight in the court of law. I had conjured a possible explanation that could cause more harm than good.

And therein lies a common dilemma of policing. The truth is not always welcome, or even cathartic. Occasionally you uncover realities so ugly and truisms so raw that you want to turn the rock back over and bury them back into the good earth forever.

It's an often overlooked aspect of being a cop. Human nature beguiles us. It confounds our sense of logic and comity. It's hidden potential and dark intimations are sometimes impossible to stomach, let alone comprehend. Most of us don't want to know. In fact, many of us don't have to.

But if you want to be a cop, it's part of the job.

I never talked to his daughter or shared my suspicions with his family. What good would it have done? The last thing I wanted to do was besmirch the character of man already in his grave.

But I still think about the case. Perhaps in part due to my lifelong curiosity about human nature.

Chapter Three: Poison of the Mind   **43**

Whatever motivated the detective, he took it with him. Whatever rationalization he might have conjured to justify drinking antifreeze will remain forever unknown. That's the real truism about human nature every observant cop learns. The hard truth about who we are that applies to almost everyone.

We're all capable of behaviors beyond our comprehension. The problem is, most of us don't know it.

CHAPTER FOUR:
THE LAND OF THE UNSOLVED

To me, cemeteries are strange.

That is, they jibe with my sensibilities. They don t make sense, even for a man whose career was steeped in death. I mean, I've seen enough corpses in various states of decay to know how depressing the process of decomposition can be. Even the most formidable headstone simply marks our return to the earth, nothing more.

But the truth is, cemeteries make me uncomfortable.

Not because they proffer a blunt commentary on the lives of people who have since disappeared. I'm not even unsettled by the figurative confirmation etched upon the rows of tombstones that life is shorter, much shorter, than we think. That s a lesson a cop learns pretty quickly.

No, what always throws me off kilter is the neatness. The absurd admixture of comity and mortality. The tidy plots and the porcelain vases arranged like sacred knick-knacks. That in the final equation, no matter how messy life is, we make sure it looks neat in the end. Maybe that's the point, to organize it, to give life a sense of order and permanence after the fact. To write the final chapter of a person's life in a way that belies the capriciousness of death.

But as a former homicide detective my first-hand experience belies that symmetry. I see nothing in a cemetery that reminds me of death as I've encountered it. The typical murder scene is simply chaos writ in a slipstream of blood. Death in the throes of violence is almost always a mess. It takes all the imagination and wherewithal of a good detective to bring some sense of order to a crime scene. To reveal the clues a killer leaves behind. A drop of blood, a spent bullet casing, a random fingerprint, the ciphers of a murder that rarely organizes themselves.

Which is why when I walk across the neatly trimmed grass and the symmetrical rows of headstones, I feel estranged. I'm reminded not of the dead who are remembered but of the murdered who are forgotten. Of the victims who passed from this earth, their stories untold. The cases that are left unsolved.

And there are plenty in Baltimore, thousands, in fact. Suspicious deaths, straight-up murders, violent killings whose perpetrators remains a mystery. Convenient accidents, bodies that surface in the harbor like vanilla-colored marshmallows, and even the random drug addict whose overdose ends with legs bound and a burial mound comprised of a pile of trash.

There are people who fall off buildings in the middle of the night and expire later in a shroud of plaster. Civic leaders shot in the back of the head whose deadly wounds were allegedly self-inflicted even though the lethal bullet was never found.

In fact, my co-author Stephen Janis and his former colleague Luke Broadwater completed an extensive investigation of the just how many murder cases resulted in jail time for the now-defunct *Baltimore Examiner*. They reviewed a decade of homicides stretching back to 1996.

The idea was to quantitatively assess how effectively Baltimore's criminal justice system prosecuted murder. To determine exactly how many homicides resulted in actual jail time. It was an investigation prompted by the fact that many cases supposedly closed are arrests which are never prosecuted, a classification that persists even if the charges are dropped or if the suspect is eventually exonerated. So the focus of their work was to determine just how many murders resulted in someone actually sitting in jail. In other words, was an appropriate punishment meted out that fit the crime? And what they found out was stunning.

Only one in four murder cases resulted in significant jail time. Nearly three-quarters of all killers over the spans of a decade would barely lose a day of freedom. Turns out in Baltimore city picking up gun, wielding a knife, or simply using your bare hands to snuff out a life is pretty much a consequence-free act. It was the simplest and most potent explanation for what ails the city. An unequivocal number that transcends all the political manipulation and downright lying about the rate of violent crime in Baltimore.

The truth is if you can't solve murders discussing just how effective police are in Baltimore is pointless. Usually when the city's abysmally low clearance rate comes under scrutiny the department offers excuses. Uncooperative witnesses. Exceptionally high case loads.

They even blame prosecutors, like when former City State's Attorney Patricia Jessamy announced in 2006 she would only try cases buttressed by two witnesses. It was an arbitrary rule that evinced quite a publicity storm. The press and the public interpreted the dispute as a sign that the police department and prosecutors couldn't work together.

The whole battle played out in the media as a contorted law enforcement turf war. Prosecutors declared that when, and if, to charge a killer was solely their purview. They accused police of assembling sloppy cases that were impossible to prosecute. Homicide detectives countered the states attorneys office was afraid to try all but the most inept killers. They accused prosecutors of essentially letting murderers roam the streets unfettered.

But that wasn t the real problem, not at all. In fact, it was a typical law enforcement smokescreen to mask a deeper flaw buried in sprawling bureaucracy of the city s two dominant law enforcement agencies. The real problem, the root cause of the conflict could be summed up in one word.

Incompetence.

That s right, plain, straightforward lack of skill, follow-through, and capability.

I know for a fact detectives arrest suspects with little evidence to bolster clearance rates. But I also know that prosecutors make matters worse by not working as closely with investigators as they did when I was on the force. Combine the lack of follow-through and teamwork with an ever-growing experience gap on the homicide floor and there just isn t the institutional wherewithal to put cases to bed.

Which is why I put so much effort into telling the story of the departed. Why I spent many a night away from my family, alone on the homicide floor typing reports, searching for clues, and whenever possible interviewing suspects. It was a commitment to the dead made for those left behind, because the living need to know. And not just to achieve closure for families, but to close cases and take killers off the streets. So that the worst among us can be forced to account for their crimes. And to insure that those who kill will not strike again.

But there s something more that ails the land of the unsolved. Something that stultifies a city where murder occurs unabated. A psychic toll which accompanies the litany of the unburied dead. The reason, in fact, that I m writing this book.

Like a body in a state of shock, each suspicious or violent death that remains unexplained, unsolved, or in the parlance of the state medical examiner 'undetermined,' contributes to our collective stasis. Like a relative who can t accept the passing of a loved one because the body is never found. Or a cancer that continues to grow because it has yet to be removed.

Baltimore is a city arrested by murder. We are stunted by violence and undermined by the perpetrators of it who persist in our midst. The simple fact is unsolved cases allow killers to live among us without fear. And in doing so we inherit their traits. We embody the psychic heritage of those who kill. We become the community of dysfunction and decay. The home of the The Wire. The showcase to the world of violence at its most unbridled in the so-called civilized world.

The truth is, I think the unsolved murders not only contribute to but fuel much of the dysfunction that has trapped the city in a sort of social purgatory. It's the worse type of communal secret that compounds the pain and loathing unrepentant violence engenders.

Think about it. The whole purpose of the justice system, at least from my perspective, is not to lock up pot smokers and parking ticket scofflaws. Truly, at our best, we reveal the worst among us. Meaning we unearth the most destructive. Ultimately, we segregate the violent, predatory, and anti-social.

But there's more to it. Because we also fill in the blanks, so the speak. Solving murders is socially cathartic. That's because untold stories of the dead are like a cloak around the conscience of the city. Like a web of lies that grows and expands until it engulfs the soul of the community itself. Each crime that remains unsolved becomes an untold story of malaise, a secret tale that contravenes the narrative of a city on the mend.

And in the end, despite the hand-wringing and the professions of the contrary by politicians who conspire to keep them, it's the secrets that will be our undoing. I mean, what we don't know can kill us. The murders which remain unmasked are symbols of our collective failure to heal. Each unsolved killing a piece of the puzzle of despair has built the foundation of unabated violence we live today. That's the most frustrating aspect of our penchant for letting unsolved murders linger on the books.

It's like watching a collective act-self deception, the process of lying about what truly ails us. We want them to go away, the victims and the perpetrators to vanish, even though in many respects they hold the key to our future betterment.

Which is why I've felt helpless watching as the Baltimore police department slowly dismantled its ability to investigate. Over the past decade, the department has de-emphasized investigation for militarization. I wrote a great deal about it in my first book, *You Can't Stop Murder*. In fact, nearly 17 years ago I analyzed the homicide division for then-commissioner Ed Norris. What I found then was as disturbing as what is happening now.

Back then the homicide floor was staffed with inexperienced officers who had not received adequate training. Investigations were languishing because caseloads were too high and supervisors were just as inexperienced as the detectives on the street. Equipment was outdated, and procedures and standards embraced for decades abandoned. The unit was a mess.

But things have probably gotten worse. I mean at the time the department was about to embark on its now infamous experiment with aggressive, paramilitary-style policing. Mayor Martin O'Malley had just begun the catastrophic implementation of the New York-style zero tolerance policing—a decision which lead to the arrest of nearly 100,000 people per year and an eventual million-dollar payout after both the NAACP and the ACLU filed a lawsuit alleging the strategy was illegal.

So I can only imagine the state of the homicide department now. In a sense, by dismantling the departments capability to investigate we've committed the perfect crime because we've limited our ability to learn about ourselves. How many secrets are hidden in those case files that remain unsolved? How many killers have been left to roam among us because someone didn't do their job, or worse yet, purposely let a case remain open? How many families are denied the basic, fundamental right of knowing how their loved one died? And who killed them?

It's a state of denial that compromises every facet of civic life. A communal cover-up which ferments and rots our institutions to the core. If we can't tell the truth about violent death, if we can't honestly understand the murderous among us, then it seems improbable that we can cure the other maladies that stunt the citys future growth and prosperity.

I mean, why maintain a homicide division with nearly 60 detectives at all if we don't want to solve cases? Why bother to have a police department at the cost of $500 million per year in direct costs alone if we can t complete the most basic function of law enforcement?

I understand that solving murders in a town like Baltimore isn't easy. I know for a fact that the caseload for your average detective is much higher than it should be, way higher. And I'm more than familiar with the idea that witnesses are at best reluctant.

But I also know that had the city dedicated the same resources and personnel it has to chasing low-level drug offenders to instead investigating homicides the results would probably be transformative. I mean, there probably isn't a cop in who town can't take you on a tour of the city's open-air drug markets. We know quite a bit about how people buy and subsequently abuse and buy drugs in Baltimore. The drug trade and its consequences are well cataloged and understood by all.

So why can't we figure how thousands of people were murdered? Why can't we assemble a reasonable body of evidence about the wholesale taking of hundreds of lives?

And I'm not just offering criticism. I tried to lend a hand, so to speak. In 2013, long before the Department of Justice issued a scathing report on the department citing systemic unconstitutional tactics and racist policies, we made a formal offer to former Mayor Stephanie Rawlings-Blake to devise a plan to overhaul the department. Hundreds of years of policing experience offered to the city to address those same deficiencies completely free of charge. Not a red cent. We were flatly turned down.

It was not just a frustrating rejection, but also somewhat sad. All professions, including policing, evolve over time. But sometimes intractable problems need historical context. Occasionally the practices of the past can offer solutions for the problems of the present. Which takes me back to thinking about cemeteries, and how they relate to one of my oddest unsolved cases.

Truthfully, it's an incident that still bothers me not so much because it remains a mystery, but what it revealed about our often lackluster approach to dealing with troubled cops. A patchwork system that remains just as byzantine and dysfunctional today as it was back then. And like many other bizarre crimes I have investigated, this one started a strange phone call.

"Lieutenant," one of my detectives mumbled into the phone. "We've got a body in the cemetery."

"A body in a cemetery?" I asked, waiting for a punch line.

"Yeah, a body."

"Sounds right to me," I quipped.

"I mean like a corpse leaned against a headstone. It's freakin' bizarre."

I paused, confused. Sure, we found plenty of bodies in Baltimore. Usually discarded in alleys or tossed in ditches, rarely placed next to a headstone.

"Is it a fresh body?" I asked, figuring it was the best question to float to avoid sounding stupid.

The detective didn't answer for a second. "Ah, it's wearing a dress and looks pretty decent. I mean, like buried body decent."

"You mean it's covered?"

"It's wearing a dress," he repeated.

"Like a burial gown?"

"Sort of," the detective replied.

I was still confused. Why were we investigating a body in a cemetery? "Who called it in?" I asked.

"The cemetery manager. He said someone dug her up and has been visiting her," he said, adding, "He's pretty upset about it."

There wasn't much else to say. I told the detective to gather as many details as possible: the name on the headstone in question, a statement from the manager of the graveyard, and a list of the most recent burials.

Of course, I wasn't sure if there was anything we could do. We were homicide detectives, after all. We solve murder cases, not the unearthing of corpses.

I had more than a few open killings still marked in up on the board. I had a couple of major reports to file and a few possible leads from unsolved murders that required my attention. But the idea of someone exhuming a body for no apparent reason still left me queasy. Why would anyone dig up a corpse to simply lean it up against a headstone? That's not normal behavior. Not even close.

But while I was pondering exactly what to do about it, I received another unusual call. This time from a supervisor from the Western District.

"I was told you're looking into an exhumed body."

"Ah, that's true."

"Well, I think I know who dug it up," he said. And so began one the weirdest phone conversations of my career, and later one of the most bizarre interrogations.

Turns out a cop under his command was acquainted with women named on the headstone–that is, before she became a corpse. A patrolman who he suspected had something to do with digging a body out of the ground and propping it up against a headstone.

"He's not a bad guy," he told me. "But I guess that's not the issue."

This particular cop had women troubles, his supervisor told me. Problems he was not shy about telling anyone who would listen. "Yeah, he's married, sort of," the commander explained. "But the rumor is his wife brings men home to sleep with right in front of him.

"The strange thing is he talks about it."

The cop in question was a good police officer with a relatively unblemished record. So it wasn't like the guy had been manifesting bad behavior. And of course, just having a difficult spouse didn't explain the body in the cemetery. I mean, cops and screwed up marriages are like beer and pizza, you can t have one without the other.

Then again, the idea that a cuckolded cop was busy digging up corpses had other less appetizing implications.

"What are you saying?" I asked. "Was this a perverted act?"

"Not exactly," the commander replied.

In fact, I recalled my detective had told me the body was clothed. Her private parts covered. She was propped up against a headstone like a person taking a nap.

"No, he's not that screwy," the commander continued, pausing. "I guess what I heard ... she was his only friend."

"Friend?" I asked.

"Yeah, she was the only woman who paid him any attention. She was like his guardian angel," he said, adding, "Word is he couldn't live without her, so he dug her out so he could talk to her."

"Talk ... to a corpse?"

The commander told me the corpse was a former neighbor who offered kind words and friendship to the spurned officer. He said this particular officer had grown dependent on the much older woman for companionship as his marriage disintegrated.

She would visit the cop, cook his meals, discuss his failing marriage and listen. She was patient, attentive, and supportive. She was like a surrogate wife. Or maybe the wise and saintly old grandmother he never had. In fact, they were intimately involved to the point where they would huddle in the bathroom to sort out his mess of a love life, at least according to the officer's estranged wife. The truth is, she was the only woman who would give him the time of day, and it seems when she died he wasn't willing to let her go.

"He lost it after she passed."

"You think he dug her up?"

"That's the theory; he needed someone to talk to."

Wow. It was beyond strange, a little sad, and creepy. I mean, I lost my wife almost eight years ago. Her name was Honey. We were happily married for more than fifty years. Not a day goes by when I don't think about her. Not a single moment when the memory of the most beautiful woman I ever laid eyes on doesn't stir in my heart. But as painful as it was to lose her, I still can't understand why this guy did what he did. It was disrespectful, odd, and downright crazy.

And that's where I entered the picture.

Because if there's one thing a good police department should just do, it's to make sure people who carry guns and wear badges are mentally sound. You can't vest whackos with arrest powers and hand them lethal weapons. I mean, a crooked cop is problematic, but at least he might be rational about his criminality. A crazy cop is a whole other animal, like a stick of dynamite attached to a book of matches.

Which is why I decided that even though disturbing a grave is a relatively minor crime in a city where putting someone in one is more prevalent, we needed to get a handle on a guy who dug one up.

It wasn't a matter of harassing or nitpicking a beleaguered cop. Investigating a cop who had potentially unearthed a body wasn't an example of internal affairs bearing down on an already overwhelmed or depressed law enforcement officer. It was a matter of public safety. I didn't want a guy who was testing out the deep end of the pool administering law and order. And if, as it appeared, this guy truly was off his rocker, I wanted to make sure he was getting the help he needed.

So I talked to him.

Chapter Four: The Land of the Unsolved   **55**

One of the lessons you learn when you sit across the table from suspected perpetrators is that there are several archetypical personalities which populate the spectrum of aberrant behavior. The innocent, as I've stated before, tend to be emphatic. They bristle at any accusation.

The truly guilty, the sociopaths, are stone-faced. This particular officer was neither. He was at best perplexed, humble, ostensibly confused and little dazed, but not defensive in the least. Like he was caught inside the cloud of intractable depression. His answers to my questions were terse and abrupt, his eyes glazed and disoriented. He behaved from the onset of our talk both distant and confused.

In fact, as I said before, our primary concern was to make sure he was relatively sane. It was more of mental health check than an interrogation.

But despite letting him know from the beginning that we weren't trying to ruin his career, the officer was not exactly cooperative. In fact, he would barely admit to having any relationship with the women in question.

"So the detective told me you used to help her to the bathroom?" I asked.

"The morning she was ill she called to help her to the bathroom. That was the only time," he replied nonchalantly.

"There were times when you sit down and have a conversation with her?"

"Yes."

"Did you ever had a conversation with her in a bathroom?"

"No, never."

In part, I couldn't believe I was asking these questions. At the time, the city was notching 300 murders a year. It was reminiscent of the equally absurd investigation into the death threat against former Commissioner Donald Pomerleau. That probe was based entirely on a joke told among fellow cops during a bitter strike in 1974 about dropping Pomerleau from a helicopter. The joke ended up in an official memo and then on my desk (a story I recount in painful details in my previous book, *You*

Cant Stop Murder). This time, though, I was trying to get a guy to admit he dug up the body of a friend because he missed her. It was hard for me to decide which investigation was more ridiculous.

"Now, this is not a sadistic type thing," I told him. "It's just the reverse. Someone handled the body very gently and could not stand to see her taken away. Perhaps just to have one last talk with her to try to bring her back. This is the reason why we are talking to you because we know you were close. The genital parts were covered, which would indicate no sex was involved."

"I don't know anything about it," he replied.

This type of give and take went on for a while. I would ask a series of innocuous questions to persuade him to fess up, and he would rebuff me with dismissive answers and matter of fact responses. Finally, after I had exhausted almost every strategy to guide him towards confession, I let him know my interest was not solely on solving a crime. I told him without hesitation that we were, in fact, trying to help him.

"We just don't want you to get the wrong idea why we are talking to you. If at any time you change your mind and sit down and think things over, don t run from it, there are people who can help you.

"We did not come here to embarrass you or anything," I added.

But the officer was silent. He agreed to take a lie detector test and then asked if he could leave. What could I say? How much further could I explore this odd line of questioning?

That was the last time I saw him or even talked to anyone about the case. I guess I wrote it off as one of those incidents that reveal some of the unacknowledged ills that afflict police. A case that demonstrates how the pressures a cop faces can build and manifest itself in the form of odd and often troubling behavior.

I don't want to trivialize what he did. It was weird, gross and disturbing. And I dont want to suggest that only cops suffer from on-the-job depression and occupational discontent. But I can at least understand the isolation and loneliness that comes with policing and how it can prompt a person to manifest aberrant behavior.

Witnessing the worst aspects of human nature on a daily basis can overwhelm the psyche. Standing over the decomposing body of a child on a hot summer day. Comforting a grieving mother after her son was shot down on a corner in a random act of violence. Attending to the dying at the scene of a fatal car accident. Being a constant and willing participant in the ongoing continuum of death and destruction takes a toll, believe me.

And since these experiences are far outside the purview of most people, it can be hard to find someone who understands the profound impact of them. It can be isolating and lonely, and maybe that's why I didn't pursue the case.

Still, I think about it occasionally, especially when I hear about another cop gone bad who commits an inexplicable act. I often wonder if police departments weren't so rigid about mental illness, perhaps if we were a little more proactive about the psychological health of cops, we could prevent many of the problem arrests and unjustified shootings that make national headlines.

I've always been a big supporter of unfettered access to mental health treatment for officers. I think there should be an open-door, no-retribution policy. I know it sounds dicey. How can we give cops psychological treatment without using the results? How can we overlook certain conditions, like depression or bipolarity, when we decide who gets to carry a gun and who doesn't? We can't simply let mentally ill people work the streets, correct?

Perhaps. But then maybe we need to consider a preventive model, because most of the mental trauma that ultimately influences the behavior of police officers worsens over time. Afflictions that may treatable at first, but become overwhelming without help. So I think by having a more progressive policy by letting police know they can get treatment with no questions asked would, in the long run, do more to prevent bad behavior than the policies in place now.

It's something we should consider in light of what ails us presently. Something I think about when my mind wanders back to this story of a lonely cop who exhumed a body. He was a man in pain, like many others. And pain untreated can often be inflicted upon the community which ignores it.

CHAPTER FIVE:
THE BIGGER THE LIE, THE BIGGER THE MESS

Only in such extremes does one become aware of how every person is lost in himself beyond hope and rescue, and one's sole consolation in this is to observe other people and the law governing them and everything.

Franz Kafka - Diaries (1914-1923)

Why do we tell stories about ourselves that are untrue? Why do we exaggerate our achievements and downplay our failures? And why do we, in moments of conversation and exchange, conflate the facts that define our lives to fit the expectations of others?

The answer may seem obvious, but its not.

Self-deception is as human as dying. It defines us, and in some ways sustain us too. We lie to temper embarrassment, or to avoid responsibility for misdeeds. We lie to bolster our achievements. And we lie to impress others. It's as richly varied human trait as natural as the stories of mayhem and violence that fill this book.

As you can imagine, lying is a bit of an obsession for me. Throughout my career as a homicide detective, I spent a good deal of time trying to figure out why people lie, and even more important, when. And during of my study of the pathology of untruthfulness, I was exposed to some of the most masterful liar's humanity has ever produced.

I have a sat across interrogation tables from hundreds of suspects who lied without pretense or conscience. I have looked into the eyes of people who committed cold-blooded murder, psychopaths who denied their role in the brutal slayings as calmly as a heart surgeon places a stent on a blood vessel.

I patiently observed as they dispassionately deflected every line of inquiry like a blind man brandishing a fly swatter. I watched, stupefied, as they displayed a matter of fact cool detachment facing the prospect of the rest of their life in prison. Men who had committed despicable acts who didn t emit a drop of sweat under the pressure of intense interrogation.

Conversely, I've witnessed innocent people cry, sputter, and otherwise fall apart when asked even the most oblique question. I watched them offer up confessions to crimes they didn t commit just to the stop the process of interrogation. People who haven t committed a single malevolent act crumble into mush after asked to simply spell their name.

Contrasting behaviors that prompted me to examine not just why people lie, but how. And what those lies reveal about the person who tells them.

Of course, you might be thinking, Tabeling, you re a cop, not a philosopher. Why do you fill your books with musings on topics that seem far removed from policing? What s the point of drilling down on a subject that s better left to psychologists? Stick to the facts and keep it simple.

Well, first of all, the whole purpose of the book is to offer a perspective beyond simple narratives of crimes. What s the point of writing a cop book just to tell a bunch of dusty old war stories without some meditation on the essence of human nature? And second, I am a student of policing, not just a practitioner. Meaning I like to delve into the murky impulses of the human psyche. Peek under the hood for a glimpse at the engine of the mind. How it works, and occasionally why it breaks down.

And from this perspective, I have learned a simple lesson about lying. A rule that I have cited more than once but will repeat: the innocent act guilty and the guilty act innocent. Not always, but quite often. It's an observation I cannot scientifically affirm, but certainly a behavior I've encountered during countless investigations.

Why?

Perhaps a man who has taken the life of another human turns cold, the decision to murder emotionally cathartic and ultimately curative of the limitations of a normal human conscience. And conversely maybe the innocent lack the resolve to face the simplest queries because they are in fact innocent. People who have never confronted the dark intimations of human savagery to the liberating extent that makes murderers so distinctly immune to self-doubt.

Of course of all the most purposeful strategies for deception, the most common tactic is also the easiest to understand: lying to hide guilt. The motivation is clear. Who wants to go to jail? And who wants to tell a cop they committed murder? Very few people, I can assure you.

But there are other types of lying that don't fit neatly into the categories of self-preservation or evasion. Fibbers who reach far beyond the practicalities of keeping up appearances, or dissuading a lover that you're having an affair to hide the truth that you are.

There are lies we share for the sake of then. Lies we tell ourselves. Exaggerations we cultivate to augment our most ambitious works of fiction; ourselves. And in some cases, that narrative like a conceptual piece of art far exceeds the reality we inhabit. Instead, we invoke imaginary deeds and conjured accomplishments that swell beyond any notion of truth.

How do I know? Because I investigated a pretty big case, a murder investigation no less, based entirely on an inexplicable lie told by a cop.

Chapter Five: The Bigger the Lie, The Bigger The Mess   **63**

A single twisting of the truth that dragged both of us into the wake of a notorious murder case. A spectacular prevarication which put me in the unenviable position of having to beg my superiors not to charge a man with murder because of an off-hand remark uttered over a hot coffee and a stale donut.

And I assure you, I'm not exaggerating. It was indeed a case that involved coffee, donuts, a hypnotist, a lie detector test and cop with a big mouth and a penchant for lying that would make Pinocchio's nose visible from space.

Tragically, it was also an investigation that started with a horrible tragedy: the grisly murder of two young girls.

During the summer of 1973, a motorist exiting I-695, known as Baltimore's beltway, noticed what he thought were bodies lying in a grassy knoll next to the off ramp. Soon investigators were on the scene staring at the remains of two young teens: Peggy Pumpian and Kathleen Cooke. Both shot in the head execution-style.

The case attracted quite a bit of attention. The girls were young, pretty, and their murders brutal. Their untimely deaths consumed the nightly newscasts and even garnered national attention. The fact that no one was immediately arrested for the crime only heightened the public's fascination with the case, and put pressure on investigators to solve it.

Which is where I came in. I was working in homicide at the time. The bodies were found in Baltimore County, so initially it seemed unlikely the case would end up on my desk.

That is, until something bizarre happened.

It was a phenomenon I had become accustomed to. Simply put, over time my career began to adhere to a casework version of Murphy's Law. If it's weird, odd, or simply outlandish, give it to Tabeling. I'm not sure why and when it started. But it seemed midway through my tenure as a homicide investigator the crazier the case, the more likely the file folder would land on my desk.

So when I got a call about city cop who was under suspicion for being the so-called 695 killer, I wasn't skeptical, just a bit wary. The top brass wanted to me investigate. And once again, I was tasked with probing the possibility a police officer had committed an atrocious crime. And again, I was being thrown headfirst into the case without warning or choice.

But it wasn't just the odd connection between that crime and a Baltimore city cop that made me anxious. It was the moment I sat down in the deputy commissioners office for my first briefing on the details of the investigation that precipitated the feeling of dread I often felt when a case seemed fraught with peril from the onset.

The lead came from state police. And there s no other way to write other than to write it: based upon a tip they received about a conversation between two men, a civilian and a city cop in a donut shop. I'm not kidding.

According to the witness, the duo was exchanging stories over coffee at the D&D in a Maryland suburb called Randallstown. The witness was talking about an armed robbery that recently occurred at a McDonald s located down the street. But then halfway through the conversation, the cop made an incredible claim.

"You know the 695 killer, he asked me," the man recounted to investigators. "They aren't going to catch him." Why not? "Because I did it. I shot them. I shot the girls."

At first the witness said he was incredulous. He thought the man was exaggerating.

"I said, nice joke, what else you got?"

"I'm serious," the alleged murderer said. "I thought about committing suicide, but I can t. I don t like what they do to bodies in the morgue."

"You're kidding right?" the witnessed pressed the confessional cop.

But the officer was insistent.

"They'll never catch him because I did it. And they'll never catch me."

The witness was so shaken that when the conversation ended, he jotted down the license plate number of the confessor. And then he called state police. And they called my deputy commissioner. And he called me.

Why?

Because as I already mentioned, that license plate belonged to a Baltimore police officer. That's right, a cop working in the central district. An unexceptional patrolman turned suspect in one of the most sensational murders in Maryland history. And now, thanks to a donut shop confession, he was my problem.

And as you can imagine, it was a dicey situation.

Like I said before, fate seemed to put me first in line whenever something crazy, unexpected, or politically trenchant needed handling. Maybe I was the guy who wouldn't complain. Or the cop who habitually kept his mouth shut. I'd like to think I was good at my job.

But who knows?

The deputy commissioner briefed me about the case in his office. The state police were anxious he told me, they believed the alleged confession was a solid lead. The case had gone cold. There was public fear to consider. They wanted a suspect, and for now, they had one: a BPD cop.

And the deputy commissioner was anxious too. I could always tell. The impassive stare as he delivered my orders with a steady, business-like voice. It all belied nervousness. And of course, his usual admonition when a case was particularly sensitive:

"Don't screw this up, Tabeling."

Thanks, I thought at the time. Just the vote of confidence I needed.

So with few details other than a coffee-fueled confession, I made a call to the central district command. I informed them I needed to arrange a sit down with the officer, now a suspect in a brutal murder. The odd thing was, his supervisor seemed nonchalant about it. I was confused.

"This pretty serious," I told him. "The state police are convinced he's a prime suspect."

"Anyone else I d be worried," he said. "But this guy likes to tell tall tales, the taller the better. So I'm not surprised."

"I take you don t think he did it?" I asked.

"Yeah, he did. And he's Charles Manson, too. Add in a few more while you re at it. Maybe he s a serial killer," the supervisor chuckled.

Wow. I was sort blown away. I know cops liked to brag about exploits and self-described heroics, but a guy taking credit for the murder of two teenage girls who hadn't committed the crime? Really?

What was in it for him?

At the beginning of this chapter I wrote about the myriad of motivations for lying: self-preservation, avoidance of punishment, the desire not to hurt the feelings of others. But if the commander was painting an accurate psychological portrait of the cop in question, then perhaps I was dealing with an entirely different type of impetus for fibbing.

So I arranged for the self-described sociopath to be transported to district headquarters.

When I entered the interrogation box, he already looked broken, not like a slick talker. His hair was tousled. His uniform askance. A three-day-old stubble peppered with hints of gray dotted his face. His shaggy eyebrows arched like rabid inchworms as he spoke. It didn t take long for him to fess up.

"I was lying," he told me when I asked him about the conversation at the donut shop." I made it all up."

"Why would you do that?" I replied, curious and a bit incredulous. "Why would you confess to a murder you didn't commit?"

"I don't know," he stammered. "We were just telling stories and I got carried away."

"Well, you're in a good deal of trouble," I countered. "The state police think you're the main suspect. And so does the deputy commissioner. And I think the reason they all believe you are is for a very simple reason: you said you did it. Why would you do that?"

"I don't know. I guess I always want to have the best story. He was telling some good stories, and I had to outdo him."

I sat stunned for a moment. If what he said was true, I was in charge of a murder investigation prompted solely by the braggadocios of a cop telling bald-faced lies in a donut shop to win an impromptu game of liar's poker. A fraught battle of narrative one-upmanship that had spiraled into something completely wacky but with possibly serious consequences.

"Are you telling me you made this all up?" I asked.

"I know, I know," he stammered. "Sometimes I exaggerate a bit."

"Well, this one was a whopper," I replied. If the disheveled cop who sat slumped in his a chair was telling me the truth, then I was dealing with an entirely different motive to fabricate. An impetus that may seem odd in this particular case but is perhaps the most common catalyst for inexplicable exaggeration: ego.

The all-too-familiar human imperative to brag. Our seemingly insatiable need to embellish our accomplishments, both real and imagined. The hyperbolic impulse and wholly quixotic human behavior that prompts us to depict ourselves in the kindest light possible. It's an even more treacherous indulgence for police.

Egos are like psychic bulletproof vests for cops. We bolster them to deflect the slings and arrows that naturally arise from a job that requires arrests, enforcing laws, and occasionally violence. A cop and his or her ego can literally bust down doors and deflect proverbial bullets. And, as was seemingly the case here, get them into a hell of a lot of trouble.

Of course, at that moment I also had to consider the possibility that he could be lying. That he was, despite his confession to the contrary, the murderer.

Ironic, right? Ironic that I was trying to decide if a self-admitted pathological liar who fibbed about committing a murder was telling the truth. It was one of those absurd dilemmas that often arise during the utterly unpredictable process of policing. How to sort out the facts of a case based solely upon the statements of a suspect who treats the truth like a shot of liquor to be downed quickly but never tasted.

At that point, I decided to stop the interrogation. I wanted to size him up. Give him a chance to elaborate, so to speak. It's not a technique, just at that moment an instinctive gut reaction to his obvious character flaws. If he was conjuring tall tales, I wanted to see how we would respond under the pressure the silence.

He didn't exactly cave, but he did open up a bit. After a couple of minutes of me simply staring across the table he offered to prove it. That is, provide evidence that he was lying about the murder, but telling the truth about the fact he was lying.

Absurd.

"I'll take a lie detector test, whatever you want," he said, running his hand through a thinning ball of hair that at the moment was standing nearly vertical. "Whatever you want me to do, I'll do it."

So I bit.

"Can we get hair samples, and do a blood test?"

"Yeah, like I said, anything you want."

"And what about your service weapon, we want it too?"

"Whatever it takes."

"You're doing this willingly?"

"Yeah ... like I said, whatever it takes."

It was an intriguing moment. Watching an apparent world-class braggart turn supplicating and humble. A bold teller of tall tales suddenly remorseful and cooperative. His performance, as unlikely as it seems, was so seemingly earnest I knew he was telling the truth.

As I said earlier, stone cold killers are smooth liars. They don't break or capitulate or volunteer any information. Or better yet agree to a lie detector test. But even more important, they rarely unravel. Whatever psychological problem prompted him to make the absurd claim he was notorious murderer had lapsed. Now he was naked and afraid. A man frantically searching for a way out of a predicament of his own careless making.

Ego. It's quite a disease.

"Alright," I said. "Let's get you hooked up."

I already had a pretty good sense where this case was going: nowhere. At that point, based on his statements I was sitting across from a bad liar, not a killer. But the deputy commissioner had a different opinion. And so did the state police. And when the deputy commissioner wants a case investigated, you proceed even if you think it's a dead end.

Which meant blood work first, ballistics test, hair samples, and finally a lie detector examination.

The blood types matched. Blood found underneath one of the girls fingertips was O positive. And the cop, unfortunately for him, was O positive too. That didn't help. Bear in mind roughly 48 percent of the population is O positive, so it wasn't conclusive. But it did feed into the perception of the top brass that the now remorseful central district cop was a legitimate suspect.

The ballistics did not. His gun, although it was the same caliber, was not the weapon used to kill the girls. His hair samples came back negative as well. A batch of contradictory evidence that offered a glimmer of hope I could prove he wasn't the guy, but not enough to convince my boss he wasn't.

Next, we conducted the lie detector test. A tool we used sparingly mostly because lie detector results aren't admissible in court. And I think with good reason.

Lie detectors compare the variations in physiological responses to different types of questions. An examiner begins the test by asking a control question he or she knows the subject will answer truthfully, for example: what's your name? Based upon the physiological response to the control question the examiner creates a baseline by measuring your blood pressure, pulse, and skin conductivity.

Later during the examination, he or she will ask a direct question about the crime: did you kill two girls and dump their bodies on the side of a highway? If the subjects physiological responses exhibit a pattern that diverges from the control question, then the theory is the subject is lying.

The problem is that lying is an innate ability with varying capability. The capacity to lie is like many human talents in that respect. I've known many a hardened criminal who could beat a lie detector test. Some people just have nerves of steel. And conversely, I've known innocents who fail regardless of how innocent they are. The lie detector test is a beatable system which presents itself as irrefutable science, and that always made me nervous.

Still, like I said, we use it. If only to assess a suspect's willingness to be scrutinized. Anyone who voluntarily agrees to be tested, it stands to reason, has less to hide than someone who won't.

Not always true, but mostly true.

But it didn't work out as I'd hoped. The results were inconclusive. Not an unusual outcome, but certainly not helpful in this case. Evidently, his talent for lying didn't hold up well under scrutiny.

As a result, the Deputy Commissioner upped the pressure to charge him. I can't say I blamed him at the time. The blood types matched. And we had an oddball confession. Even though I repeatedly told the police commissioner I thought the guy was innocent; he apparently didn't trust my conclusion. He wanted the case closed. So we came up with an idea. I know this sounds offbeat, but we were desperate. Don't get me wrong; I wasn't advocating for this guy. I wasn't his defense attorney. He made his own ugly bed.

But what bothers me more than a stupid cop who can't shut his mouth is an investigator wasting time pursuing the wrong man.

No one, and I mean no one, I ever worked with wants to put the wrong guy in jail. It's just not the way a good detective is hardwired. Once you've sat in court and watched a case unfold you get a sense of the implications of making a mistake. Once you've witnessed a judge send a human being to jail for decades, it's sobering. You don't want to get it wrong. The consequences are simply too profound.

Even worse, focusing on the wrong suspect and tracking down bogus leads distracts from finding the actual culprit.

So we called a hypnotist.

I know what you're thinking. What a crock. Why would consulting a hypnotist provide any less or more reliable analysis than a lie detector test? If a seemingly scientific method for detecting deception isn't admissible in court what on earth could you accomplish using a hypnotist?

It's a worthwhile question. Let me try to answer.

Technically the hypnotist is a human lie detector without the aid of the aforementioned physiological cues. The hypnotist mines the subconscious using techniques that make the subject both self-aware and unconscious simultaneously. The idea is to relax the conscious defenses, the natural barriers that block unfettered truth telling. Or remove the psychological obstacles to distinguish between what happened versus what we think happened.

It's not a precise science. And it relies quite a bit on subjective analysis. But I trusted the hypnotist we hired. I'd engaged him before, and he always offered both a useful and frank assessment. Nothing overly precise or too definitive. Just a straightforward analysis accompanied with reasonable caveats. I liked to call it a 'spectrum' of truthfulness.

He didn't pretend to have the final word on the forthrightness of the subject. He simply offered a professional opinion based upon his observations. It was like a supplement to my analysis, and almost always useful.

So I asked the increasingly desperate patrolman if he would try hypnosis. Like I already said, the upper echelon of both the BPD and the state police were breathing down my neck. And none of the evidence thus far had provided adequate proof to convince them he was anything but guilty. Hypnosis was the proverbial Hail Mary, not a total act of desperation but an attempt to obtain an alternate perspective. An objective opinion that I could use to make my case that our befuddled cop was not a murdering nutcase.

Fortunately, he agreed.

I was present during the hypnosis. It was standard practice for us to observe. We'd, of course, reviewed the doctor's approach before the appointment. We'd thoroughly checked out his credentials with other law enforcement agencies. I understand hypnosis isn't necessarily a mainstream policing technique, but you'd be surprised how many investigators turned to it during the 1970s. Remember, we didn't have DNA testing, for example, or many of the so-called CSI technologies. We had to find other ways to wrangle the truth.

The cop was given a series of directions. Cues accompanied by deep breathing and concentration exercises along with simple commands associated with them. It wasn't like snap your fingers and stand up and walk. The session was conducted with a more nuanced set of directives. A methodical soothing of the natural defenses of the mind to open the conscience and pave the way unfettered recall.

"He opened up completely," the hypnotist said after the session was over. "He was very susceptible."

And his assessment? Exactly what I expected.

"My professional opinion, he was lying," the hypnotist told me. "He has no recollection of the killings, and even more important, no apparent obvious feelings of guilt. Only the remorse that he lied."

"It seems highly unlikely he killed anyone. In fact, almost impossible."

It wasn't incontrovertible proof, but it was something. I had a second opinion from a respected source confirming what I suspected. The gun didn't match. Hair samples were negative. All my instincts hewn over years of investigation told me he wasn't the guy. And the hypnotist seemed equally convinced.

While I was waiting for the hypnotist's opinion, I did a little more detective work. I questioned the suspect's family about his penchant for exaggeration. His sister was extremely forthcoming.

"He's been like since he was a boy," she told me over the phone. "If you tell a story, he's got to tell a bigger one."

"Any idea why?"

"I just think he's always got to be the baddest guy in the room. I guess he can't help himself."

It wasn't new information, but relevant. Whenever you're working on a case as convoluted as this one, it helps to evince patterns; a set of basic underlying facts from independent sources. It's like when you interview witnesses at the scene of a shooting. All their stories will vary in one way or other. But there will be a particular set of indelible facts they all agree upon. I call it communal pattern recognition. And in this case several independent sources converged on the same irrefutable pattern: my story-telling cop was a pathological liar, not a killer.

Unfortunately, my array of character witnesses and hypnosis didn't impress the deputy commissioner. I was summoned to his office for an update. He wanted the braggart charged. And at the very least, held in detention.

"Sir, I don't think that's a good idea."

"I'm not asking your opinion, Tabling."

"If I hold him, I have to charge him, and since I don't have enough evidence to charge him, we'll have to release him eventually." I explained to the deputy commissioner how bad that would look. How holding, charging, and then ultimately dropping the case against a cop formally accused of being the 695 killer would appear like we botched the investigation. Even if we had suspicions, there just wasn't enough evidence to prosecute a case in court. Despite his impromptu confession, there was scant evidence that we could bring to trial. And for all those reasons, I strongly advised against doing anything.

"Just hold him, then."

"On what basis?" I asked.

The deputy commissioner stared across his desk. He wasn't the type of man who appreciated pushback. It was clear he was taking heat from state police. And he didn't want to come up empty handed; particularly when we had a cop who had already confessed to the crime.

"I want you to hold him," he repeated.

"I think that's a mistake."

"I'll say it again. I'm not asking, Tabeling."

It was one of those no-win moments all too common in policing. My investigation had not produced the results command expected. And worse, I faced the unpleasant dilemma of having to defy a superior or do something I knew was simply wrong.

I convinced the deputy commissioner to let me call the prosecutor who was handling the case. The idea was to check with him before we did anything. The truth is, if he didn't think the evidence warranted the charges, the case would be over before it began. Fortunately, the deputy commissioner reluctantly agreed.

One thing people may or may not understand is that a cop can charge someone, but the prosecutor has the final say. In other words, I can do all the arresting I want, but the prosecutor can ultimately drop the case in court if he or she doesn't think it's up to snuff. This division of law enforcement power has been a public point of conflict in Baltimore.

For example, as I recounted in the previous chapter, former Baltimore State's Attorney Patricia Jessamy made headlines when she publicly stated she would only charge murder cases that involved two witnesses. It was an absurd statement, a blanket judgment that contradicts the complexity and intricacy of murder investigations. Successfully solving murders requires flexibility. I once solved a case without a body, let alone a witness.

But that conflict also demonstrates the critical role prosecutors play in the outcome of any investigation. They are both the check and balance on what we do. They are the final arbiter on whether a case goes to court, and if and when charges are leveled. That's why I always worked closely with the state's attorney's office. If I had questions, I asked. If I needed advice on the law, I sought them out.

And this time I needed more than advice, I needed a sound legal mind to help me convince the deputy commissioner this case could not go forward.

So I called the state's attorney who would ultimately be responsible for prosecuting the cop if it ended up in court. I reviewed the evidence with him. I recounted what I had, and what I didn't. I provided him an overview of the hypnotist's opinion, the results of the lie detector test, the blood work, ballistics, and hair analysis.

"Steve, I don't think we have the makings of a case," he said after I'd finished. "We can't charge him."

"I know, but the commissioner wants me to hold him."

"On what basis?"

"I don't know; I can't think of any good reason. Personally I believe he's feeling the heat from the state police."

"Let me talk to him," the prosecutor offered.

And he did. He explained that the state's attorney's office was not prepared to charge the cop with anything, let alone murder. And that holding him without charges was illegal. Ultimately he informed the none-too-happy deputy commissioner that the case was weak at best, silly at worst.

The BPD's second in command reluctantly agreed charges were not warranted. What could he do? The prosecutor had the final say. Thanks to that phone call, I didn't have to charge the cop with a single crime. It was a relief, for me, and not the last time an able prosecutor in the state's attorney's office bailed me out of sticky situation. I was, to say the least, grateful. I met with the voluble officer to inform him of the decision. He was relieved, even a bit chastened.

"Thanks," he professed. "Thanks for looking out."

"Don't thank me," I replied. "There was no evidence."

But the case was far from over. Sadly, avoiding spurious charges didn't bring the murderer to justice.

About a year later I received a call from the state police. They'd arrested the killer of the two girls. And it was more bizarre, twisted and sick than even I could imagine.

The killer was a man named Charles Davis, Jr. He was the son of a Baltimore County police lieutenant. He was also a part-time ambulance driver. He would stalk his victims, observing them for hours before abducting, strangling, and raping them. Even worse, he would dump his victim's bodies in a public place and then call 911 so he could respond to the scene of his crime. In the end, he abducted and murdered five women. And in almost all the cases, he visited the murder scene in his capacity as an EMT, or emergency medical technician.

He was caught after a state trooper pulled him over for driving with stolen tags. The trooper found a CB radio in the car that was also stolen. An investigation determined the radio was purchased with a credit card lifted from a rape victim who, incredibly, survived his attack. Later she identified Davis as her assailant, and he was charged with forcible rape.

Davis, however, fled to Nevada. After he had been extradited back to Maryland to face the rape charges, he asked to speak privately with the trooper transporting him. In the back seat of state trooper's cruiser, he was advised of his rights, and then confessed to killing Peggy Pumpian and Kathleen Cooke.

The arrest provided little consolation for me. I was relieved that we had not put the wrong man behind bars. Even if he was a cop who couldn't tell the truth, he didn't deserve to be charged for a crime he didn't commit. As for the deputy commissioner, he never said a word about it.

But the simple fact remains that all of it was a horrible tragedy. Beyond my personal relief that we hadn't blown a major investigation, there still were five families who had lost loved ones. Victims who died the worst sort of sudden and violent death. And a complete sicko and deranged personality who had masqueraded as a first responder while terrorizing the state for months.

Still, I think this case taught me a lesson that still applies to my work today. Lying is not a behavioral trait that can be whittled down into an exact science. Its a creative art as unpredictable and unwieldy as any other human predilection. A capability we all possess, but like other talents, exercise with varying degrees of ability. And most important, a behavior that comes with all the diverse array of capacities and capabilities that make human beings so interesting.

And dangerous.

CHAPTER SIX:
SEX IN OUR CITY

Let me be frank: I'm a cop. Not a philosopher.

I'm a hardscrabble guy of blue-collar roots who worked the streets of a city with a temperament akin to reinforced steel. A land where few are forgiven and vengeance is an ingrained reflex.

But that doesn't mean I've eschewed turning to the other ways of thinking about crime and law enforcement when it seems appropriate. I'm a compulsive reader and seeker of knowledge and wisdom. I continue to explore news ways of thinking about policing to benefit my profession and the people I serve. Which is why occasionally during my career I've turned to philosophy to inject some context into the discussion of how and why we police.

I admit policing and philosophy seem like two diametrically opposed topics. Policing, at its most basic, is raw and physical, adrenalized and immediate. Even as you rise through the ranks towards less physical administrative and investigative positions, the mentality of being prepared to confront the random violence and unexpected chaos never fully recedes. You are, to be truthful, always mindful of the potential for bad things to happen.

Philosophy, on the other hand, is more a cerebral preoccupation. An intellectual excursion into the meaning of life, why we exist, and other existential questions that I became a cop to avoid.

But I've always tried to gain perspective on my profession from unlikely sources. It's one of the reasons I earned several advanced degrees from Loyola College in psychology. I wanted to be exposed to different ways of thinking so I could contrive new ways of thinking about policing. And let's face it–law enforcement is a profession that needs it. Now more than ever.

During this pursuit, I came across a famous German philosopher you may already be familiar with: Friedrich Nietzsche. He's a controversial 19th-century thinker who continues to confound contemporary critics with his insights into human nature, but nonetheless prompted me to reconsider my assumptions about both people, policing, and how both interact.

Nietzsche is, of course, best known for his idea of the Uber Man, an intellectually and physically superior human being who transcends morality with the sheer force of human will.

But Nietzsche appealed to me for a much more straightforward reason. I consider him to be one of the first and foremost genuinely compelling psychologists. Many of his philosophical musings focus upon the examination of the root cause of human behaviors and the contradictory impulses the mind elicits.

Which is why I occasionally like to consult his work. He contemplates, albeit indirectly, one of the great dilemmas of policing: how does a community, and in my case an individual, deal effectively with bad behavior? And why, despite all the disincentives we have erected, do a certain number of people inevitably break the law?

Nietzsche had a theory about civilization that in my opinion partly addresses this question. He said that all societies were governed by two contradictory impulses. One he called the Apollonian, the upstanding, quotidian, human desire for continuity and cooperation. Our impetus to build functional civilizations. Put simply, the nearly ideal version of society where things run smoothly and humanity works towards collective betterment.

He also posited the opposite of the Apollonian: the Dionysian. It represents our hedonistic, sexual, and otherwise escapist impulses. Our lascivious sexual desires, our need for carnal release, all the chaotic and unpredictable behavior of human beings corralled into a single concept.

The idea is based upon the characteristics of two Greek gods: Apollo and Dionysius. Both were the offspring of Zeus, but like many families, the siblings' personalities and backstories were conflicted.

Apollo was the god of music, poetry and fine art. He was also adept at healing and considered a purveyor of medicine. Symbolically speaking Apollo was represented by the sun and sunlight.

Dionysius, on the other hand, had a slightly different temperament. For one thing, he was the only god born of a mortal parent, Semele. He created wine, and along with it the ecstasy of intoxication. But he was temperamental and prone to angry outbursts, perhaps the result of his penchant for drunkenness. In fact, shortly after a jealous lover of Zeus tried to murder him, Dionysus wandered the woods with a group of lascivious women, wreaking havoc upon humans.

Nietzsche believed these two distinct gods represented many of the contradictory impulses necessary to create a vibrant human society. One could not exist without the other, Nietzsche argued, no matter how conflicted or seemingly irreconcilable either impulse could be. He believed human civilization without the benefit of both attributes would be sterile and unappealing.

And this notion of competing and contradictory impulses co-existing within the psyche of a community are applicable to the city I call home: Baltimore. My community of birth exists in a convoluted civic crossroads harboring the seemingly most austere and indiscrete manifestations of human ingenuity and destructive behavior existent.

We have great institutions like Johns Hopkins Hospital and University, a beautiful waterfront palisade known as the Inner Harbor, a storied history of civil rights movements and homegrown musical artists like the iconic and legendary jazz singer Billie Holliday.

But we are also touted as the heroin capital of the world. We are perennial stalwarts on the list of top ten of the most violent cities in the country. And today you can still walk among the remnants of one of the few remaining red light districts known as 'The Block,' where sex is openly sold on barstools for twenty bucks. An area of outright prostitution situated dead center in the city's urban core not far from its top tourist attractions.

In fact, it was on The Block that I witnessed the city's Dionysian character in all its extravagance and excess.

During the 1970s I worked in the city's Central District as a plainclothes detective and a homicide supervisor, two beats which would occasionally deposit me inside the subterranean strip of bars and Carnivalesque night clubs that populate it. During that time I investigated quite a few cases that seemed to embody all the cruel imperatives of the human sex drive, and the resulting extreme behaviors such a primitive and apparently Dionysian force elicits.

I once arrested a group of Greek seaman who had stowed women against their will aboard a tanker bound for the US. When the ship docked in Baltimore, the men delivered their captives to one of the dingiest sex establishments I had ever seen. There, ensconced down a set of smoke-stained stairs, the women were sold as sex slaves to the highest bidder. Young females who couldn't even speak English sequestered inside a dank rattrap of an establishment like just so much cattle.

I witnessed the prostitution of minors, young women sold by their mothers to lawyers and doctors in basement bars amid dirty toilets and rickety plumbing. In fact, The Block and its squalid environs were the living embodiment of the city's most troubling Dionysian character. And in many ways, it got worse over time, devolving like many of Baltimore's institutions in tandem with our unfaltering deindustrialization.

Walk the block in the 1950s and you would see not a succession of seedy bars and greasy pizza joints, but a dazzling array of Broadway-like neon-lit grand marquees. Step inside a club and you would be entertained by women in intricate costumes festooned with dazzling jewelry and mesmerizing routines. Dancers performing tightly choreographed and provocative numbers accompanied by live musicians and theatrical flair. It was a spectacle of sex, sound, and sensuality.

I'm not romanticizing the place. It was—still is, to a certain extent—a glorified brothel. But The Block back then produced superstars, not just strung out young women in search of a fix. Take, for example, Blaze Starr, who built a national reputation as an electrifying dancer performing some of the best burlesques in the country.

Still, as I already stated, the city's red light district was and always has been about sex, and of course selling it. And working plainclothes in Baltimore's Central District, invariably your beat and the city's sex trade collided. I was indeed at the nexus of the city's Dionysian impulse as it morphed from an entertainment district into the repository for deviance it is today. A place where tourists indulge fantasies for a price extracted from the city's working class female progeny. A disturbing mixture of decadence and poverty that gets uglier the closer you look.

But surprisingly, The Block was not the scene of the worst case of sexual deviancy I investigated during my career. No, the most trenchant expression of the Baltimore's penchant for vice didn't occur in the city's red light district. Instead, I found myself face to face with the most troubling example of the city's Dionysian character inside a small, South Baltimore after-hours liquor joint that not myself or fellow officers would have suspected would be home to the level of debauchery we uncovered.

The case started with a tip relayed during a conversation I had with a suspect. I was working plainclothes narcotics in the Southwest district.

My job was to stem the rising tide of illicit drugs infiltrating blue collar Baltimore neighborhoods. We were gathering intelligence on a heroin ring that had taken over half the drug trade in the area.

So we busted a petty dealer selling adulterated dope from his row home not far from what we believed to be the headquarters of an increasingly expansive drug operation. A so-called foot solider selling dime bags of heroin packed and cut just down the street.

However, like many large drug operations, the top dogs were well hidden. They pushed the risk down the supply chain by enlisting small time contractors like my informant: a guy who barely made enough to keep the lights on. And like most small-time dealers in our sector, he was an easy bust. Thats because his job was to sell, and selling drugs to all comers simply makes you vulnerable to narcotics cops.

Which is why that evening I was focused on this habitually fidgety dealer I will call Mike. We had just caught him dead to rights in a hand-to-hand buy with one of my undercover men. It was the third purchase of heroin out of Mikes cramped row home we'd made that week, enough of a haul to press charges of possession with intent to distribute. A case easily bolstered by the roughly 30 additional bags of dope we found stuffed under a cushion in his sofa.

We both sat on the threadbare couch in his living room. One of those odd moments that regularly punctuates policing: a cop and a perp sharing the same space defined by totally different realities. It was both awkward and surreal as I watched him smoke cigarettes as fast he could light them.

"You sold us enough dope to warrant a pretty hefty set of changes," I told him. "It's not looking good for you." He didn't answer immediately. Frankly, there was so much smoke in the room I couldn't tell if he was listening.

"Don t tell me," he finally replied. "How am I supposed to make a living?"

"You could always get a job."

"I had a job, but its gone."

It was not the first time I heard that particular lament. In fact, it was a common refrain in the neighborhoods that encircled and adjoined the city's fading industrial base. The stable, well-paying blue collar jobs were fast disappearing in the late '60s and early '70s. And new businesses weren't stepping in to replace them. Thus I had a bit of empathy for him, along with the other small-time peddlers I arrested as the drug trade spread across the city.

Yes, they were drug dealers, but I couldn't help thinking that circumstance had in part forced their hand. That somehow the economic collapse had stacked the proverbial deck inexorably against them.

"Listen," I said. "You're just a bit player in the scheme, not the target. Help me and I can talk to the prosecutor."

"Help you, what the hell," he paused blowing an impromptu cloud of smoke towards the ceiling. "I gotta live, I gotta eat. I'm just trying to make a living. And if I help you, I won't be around to do any of that."

Unfortunately, he was right. It wouldn't take long for word to hit the street Mike had been arrested. And if shortly after that we cracked down on the entire operation, even an idiot could figure out what happened. Still, it was his best chance.

"I understand," I said. "But anything you tell me would be confidential," I added. "Why not help yourself out and make things easier?" For a moment Mike just sat and stewed. He lit another cigarette. Fixed his eyes upon the end of the butt and inhaled deeply.

"Why are you picking on people like me and not real the criminals, I mean seriously deranged types?"

"Meaning?"

"You're wasting your time busting people like me trying to survive and letting some real sickos off the hook."

"You're selling poison to your neighbors, that's hardly innocent," I replied.

"Yeah, selling dope is a lot better than selling kids."

I was caught off guard. I wasn't expecting the discussion to veer towards the topic of pedophilia.

"Kids? Can you be a little less vague?" And then, through a halo of mentholated smoke, Mike offered a tantalizing tidbit.

"You heard of Marty's?"

"Sure," I replied. "The after-hours joint right around the corner."

"Well, it's not just a bar."

"What do you mean?"

"There's a lot more going on in there. Some sick stuff."

"Like what?"

Mike dragged down on the remains of his cigarette. He plowed the butt into a heaping ashtray. "I thought you were going to arrest me."

"I am."

"Well then, do what you gotta do," he said bluntly. "But if I were you, I'd check it out."

"A few more details would be helpful."

"Like I said, check it out. If you find anything, and you will, you owe me."

I did arrest him. There wasn't much I could do about the law. But the tip was intriguing.

I was familiar with the bar. It was an unremarkable local after-hours hangout. I checked around. It had not exhibited the usual symptoms of criminal mischief like a slew of recent liquor board complaints or significant arrests. Still, I thought it might be worth investigating. Bear in mind, after-hours clubs were always skirting the law, fueled by improvised liquor licenses and shady business practices. Not the type of enterprise we liked, but one we sometimes tolerated.

Not sure why I believed my informant. And not sure why he gave me a tip that would not do him much good with respect to the charges he was facing. Perhaps that's what made it an intriguing tip. Maybe he relayed the information out of good faith. Maybe Mike had a moral center.

Of course, if there was some bad stuff happening inside that bar, we couldn't just barge in and flash our badges. We needed to infiltrate unnoticed. Survey the landscape without raising suspicion. Put some undercover cops inside to get an unfiltered look behind the scenes. And to make both strategies work, we turned to the liquor board.

In Baltimore, like many cities, liquor inspectors have the right to visit any establishment without a warrant. And that right, stipulated in all liquor licenses, extends to cops. So one night, with a liquor inspector in tow, we paid Martys a visit. It was a classic corner Baltimore after-hours joint. A watering hole situated on the intersection of two Southeast District streets. Sort of the like the period at the end of a run-on sentence. The type of establishment that populated a large southern swathe of the city.

And inside it was just as unremarkable. The bar itself was crowded. A paltry jukebox wheezed out Led Zeppelin. The stench of beer soaked into the pores of dappling rafters.

The patrons were predominantly male and stacked side-by-side. Blue-collar types, hardworking, heavy-smoking. They barely noticed us. It was, in a sense, suspiciously calm.

So I checked around. A pool table ensconced in the back served as the site of a heated green felt gladiator s match. Four men, all drunk, waved pool sticks like longswords as they jostled for position in a protean game of 8-ball.

It was wall-to-wall men. Women were scarce, to the say the least.

Something didn't smell right.

But I wasn't going to figure it out by standing around inspecting the provenance of gin bottles. I followed the inspector as he checked the liquor license to make sure it was on premises. While he reviewed liquor purchases to make sure excise fees were paid, I surveyed the crowd. Nothing appeared out of order, so we left.

But I couldn't shake the feeling there was something I hadn't seen. A vital clue I'd missed. Maybe it was the gender imbalance, which is not totally unusual for a hole-in the-wall bar, but just seemed different in this case. Maybe it was the behavior of the patrons, indifferent to our presence. Not casual diffidence, but an almost contrived nonchalance. There was something amiss, something untoward that I couldn't immediately put my finger on.

So I decided to send in one of my undercover officers. I told him to blend in and figure out what was going on. If I couldn't get a read myself, I knew an undercover cop would be the next best thing. A man in camouflage with a gun and a badge.

"Take your time with this," I told him. "Don't push it."

The first night he visited the bar he didn't have much to report, save one intriguing observation. "People would go to a back room, then leave the bar," he told me. "And then return like an hour later."

"How many?" I asked.

"About a dozen guys, it was like an assembly line. One right after another." I wasn't sure exactly what it meant, but it was a pattern. Odd behavior worth pursuing.

The typical corner bar in the district I worked was anything but transient. At least in Baltimore, bar hopping is bad etiquette. Regulars root themselves on bar stools like potted plants to be intermittently watered with booze. The rule: you drink until you drop. Then stumble home and return the next day to start all over.

"When you go back tonight, I want you to ask about where these people are going," I told him. "And if they offer to show you, whatever it is, tell them next time."

"And there will be a next time," I added.

Two days later, my undercover man emerged from the bar with an interesting lead. He had asked around about the nightly procession out of the bar. He said his fellow patrons were circumspect. But one of the bartenders posed a question that piqued his curiosity. "You lonely?" he asked. Sure, my cop replied. "If you're lonely, show up tomorrow night, and bring some cash."

It was oblique but promising. I hadn't received any reports from the vice unit about the bar. And we hadn't stumbled across organized prostitution in that particular part of the district. But the offer from a bartender was an intriguing clue that implied the establishment might not be a run-of-the-mill waterhole.

The following night we set up a more elaborate operation. Myself and two other members of the unit staked out the bar. We had an advance man parked a few blocks away in case the undercover was directed somewhere else. The entire crew was in radio contact.

We parked across the street and waited.

About an hour later, the undercover emerged. He walked briskly to his car, a furtive nod the signal we were expected to follow. It was strange, to be sure. What kind of vice scheme included an off-site operation?

I'd seen the technique used by drug dealers. Hand over the money, drive around the block and pick up the dope. But this was a different type of transaction. Pay for sex, and have sex on site. Brothels were usually one-stop shops where the pimp and prostitute work under the same roof.

So we tailed him. He took us on a tour of the town. From the depths of the Southern District onto Martin Luther King Boulevard that leads North towards midtown. Then west on Chase Street past the Meyerhoff concert hall. And finally across Mt. Royal Avenue into the heart of the city's Mt. Vernon neighborhood, proximate to the campus of the esteemed Maryland Institute College of Art.

He parked his car and entered one of the neighborhoods stately brownstones; a different type of edifice than Baltimores more modest row homes. The Mt. Vernon variety was a bit more elegant, the progeny of the city's 19th-century mercantile class. They were larger and structurally grander. Interiors embellished with intricate woodwork and stunning hand crafted staircases. Dollar for dollar Mt.Vernon row homes are the closest thing to sidewalk mansions in the city.

So again, we waited.

It didn't take long for the undercover to reappear. He looked uncomfortable, almost agitated.

We drove to the rendezvous point. A 24-hour diner across town in Southeast Baltimore. As we sat down in the booth to confer, I noticed the undercover officer was shaking a bit.

"What s wrong?" I asked.

"Two girls," he said. "Both minors."

"How old?"

"Fifteen, maybe 17. The bartender asked for cash. Gave me the address in Mt. Vernon," he recounted. "I paid and left. When I got to the apartment, a man with a key let me in the room. And there they were."

"Two minors?" I repeated.

"Not just minors," he replied. "They were..."

"What?" I asked.

"Slow ... retarded, I think. They were like little kids. It was sick."

"What?"

"They were dressed up like dolls. Lipstick, makeup. But they didn't seem aware. Like the lights were on but no one home."

"Holy cow."

"Yeah, it's a mess." The undercover gripped his coffee cup. He leaned across the table. "I told them I would be back. It was going to be ok."

I didn't say anything.

"We need to go back now, like right away, Sarge. We can't just leave 'em there."

He was right; we couldn't. Baltimore had plumbed the depths of her Dionysian spirit. Like I already mentioned, working vice you witness human behavior at its most primitive and venal. Crack-addicted strippers and pregnant heroin addicts offering ten-dollar blowjobs. Sweaty pimps and dope fiend boyfriends selling women like the cheap pizza at a 24-hour carryout. But two mentally challenged underage girls holed up in apartment sold a dozen times a night was simply a new and unfathomable low.

However, there was a problem with acting immediately.

I agreed with my undercover detective; we couldn't just leave the girls in limbo while we worked to build a case. The thought of two childlike females bearing the brunt of an endless stream of unfettered sexual predators was disturbing, to say the least. But the obstacle to acting quickly was twofold: getting a warrant after midnight and planning a raid that would keep both the victims and my officers safe while effectively ensnaring the men responsible for perpetrating the crime.

My impulse, like the undercover, was simply to drive back to the Mt. Vernon and bust the girls out. But we didn't have the legal paperwork in hand or a working plan for the raid. Without both, we could just as easily blow the case and let the people responsible walk. That is the common dilemma a cop often faces, how to serve both the law and justice at the same time.

And this case presented that conflict in the most unambiguous terms.

Do I wait and plan, or act now? Do I bust down the door and free the girls, or get the proper paperwork to execute a good search? It's not that cops can't bust down a door when they have probable cause that a crime is occurring, I just didn't want to take the risk that the search could be challenged in court. Meaning I was going to get a warrant and make sure it was done right.

I wanted to collect all the evidence I could and build the strongest case possible. Not an easy decision, but the appropriate call if you're intent on achieving the ultimate goal: putting the scumbags responsible for the crime behind bars for a long time.

Fortunately, I was both a student of law and familiar with tactical logistics, so I knew how to complete both aspects of the investigation quickly. Armed with my undercover detective's observations, I constructed two search and seizure warrants: one for the bar and the other for the Mt. Vernon apartment.

And since I had executed major search and seizure raids before, I was familiar with the manpower needed and administrative coordination necessary to execute an operation like this quickly.

But first I needed the warrant signed, and fast.

Luckily I had a made of habit getting help to write warrants. I had built relationships with some of the best judges and prosecutors in Baltimore. From them, I learned how to articulate the legal concepts necessary to write a legally sufficient and effective warrant. And it was one of those mentors who I called at 2:00 a.m. shortly after I had drafted my legal justification for raiding the two establishments without delay.

"Hello, sir, sorry to call so late."

"I assume you wouldn't be calling if it weren t important," he replied, his weary voice prompting second thoughts on my part about making the phone call.

"Yes, sir. We have a situation. Two mentally impaired underage girls are being prostituted out of an apartment in Mt. Vernon."

"That's a pretty good reason to wake up an old man."

"Yes, sir. If you wouldn t mind I would like to bring the warrant now."

"Of course, come on over."

And that was it. Not what you see on the television. The never ending continuum of obstructionist judges and indifferent prosecutors. No sign of the faceless bureaucracy who espouse ambivalence towards corralling killers and rapists as quickly as possible. I was on the judge's doorstep at 2:30 a.m where he reviewed the warrant, signed it and wished me well as I left with it in my hand 10 minutes later. Next we planned the raid.

That meant more late night calls. I quickly contacted and assembled all the plainclothes officers I could locate. I didn't tell them exactly what we were doing or who the target was. Cops gossip, and my undercover thought he had recognized a few city cops in the bar. Oblivious and drunk, but cops nonetheless. So to keep the raid clean I didn't divulge details or my plan of attack until the last possible second.

We decided to execute the search warrants simultaneously on both locations. The concern of course, that hitting one and not the other would jeopardize evidence, and most importantly, the victims.

Truthfully, I felt like I was working on a horrific deadline. Every extra minute it took to process paperwork and assemble my team translated into another victimization of two minor children. Having three daughters of my own only made the waiting worse. As a father, I just couldn't fathom the pain and horror the girls were experiencing. Their plight fueled my motivation to get the raid team assembled and to plot out a strategy that would rescue them for good in short order.

Fortunately, within 24 hours we were ready to go. Two groups of plainclothes detectives assembled at both locations. The warrants were written and approved. Uniform officers along with vans were on standby to transport prisoners. We were all set. All I had to do was give the order.

It's not a moment you savor, making the call to unleash the full and unbridled power of a police department upon a criminal enterprise. It may sound heady, but it's not. An experienced cop knows just how much can go wrong. How any act precipitated by force can lead to unexpected consequences. And just how easy it for a group of cops armed with guns to elicit a violent and unpredictable response. I just wanted everyone to be safe, particularly the victims.

So with a bit of trepidation and quick prayer I radioed both teams a simple instruction: Go. And they did. In one simultaneous act of organized chaos a team of detectives bounded up the stairs of the Mt. Vernon building while an even larger group swarmed the bar.

It was an impressive show of force and quite a surprise to the perpetrators of the crimes. In all, we netted 10 suspects from the bar. Bartenders, bouncers, two owners a couple of other hangers-on. All of them participated in one way or another in pimping the young girls.

We also uncovered an illegal numbers game. Betting slips, thousand of dollars in cash, and notebooks recounting a fairly significant illegal gambling operation. Meanwhile, the Mt. Vernon search lead to two arrests, and more importantly, the freedom of the two young victims who were still ensconced in the cramped one bedroom apartment when my officers burst through the door.

Back at the station, I briefly encountered the girls before they were transferred into the custody of social services. It was a both a deeply troubling and somewhat satisfying moment.

They weren t just young, they were devastatingly innocent. Meaning they were girls whose mental impairment made them even more vulnerable. I was only able to see them through glass. Standing in the observation room, watching them sit patiently while one of my detectives gently questioned them only raised my ire.

Yes, they exhibited the telltale signs of their disability. But the faces, their bright eyes and curious expressions evinced an openness so unfiltered I was overwhelmed. I couldn t countenance the lack of humanity of the hundreds of men who forced themselves upon them.

It was a lack of self-awareness so conspicuous it offered another ugly and all-too memorable installment in my exploration of the depths of human depravity. It was an impression I have never forgotten. A personal lifelong lesson about the often deplorable behavior of men, particularly when it comes to satiating sexual impulses. There is no bottom to it, I concluded. Just an unfathomable swamp that keeps getting murkier the further you wade into it.

We were able to glean from the victims they had been taken from their family nine months before we discovered them. Their parents both missing and presumed dead. Their alleged guardian, an uncaring relative, who was also arrested. A person who never bothered to check on the whereabouts of the two girls, apparently totally unconcerned about their collective fate.

I learned later both the girls had IQs of roughly 60. They were, in essence, children. And they did show signs of trauma. Edginess, spontaneous bouts of crying, sensitive to touch. All the symptoms of what we now call Post Traumatic Stress Disorder. But still, to a certain extent, their collective pain was unknowable. The depth of their real sorrow, the true measure of their personal anguish, was simply beyond our ability grasp. A gap in understanding that would remain stubbornly out of reach despite our best efforts to elicit some inkling of how they felt.

Fortunately, the raid netted multiple convictions with lengthy sentences for the mastermind, the owner of Marty's, and several of his henchmen. It was a good example of productive law enforcement. We had stopped the savage exploitation of innocents and shut down a criminal organization that was spreading its tendrils through a solid blue-collar neighborhood. And almost as important, sent a message to the criminal community at large: You can't operate with impunity on my watch.

But all of this success was tempered by the indelible experience of confronting the darkest intimations of the city's Dionysian psyche. It is, I guess a more sobering rendering than Nietzsche might have had in mind when he delineated the conflict between Apollo and Dionysus as somehow representative of the contravening imperatives of a community. His idea that the exploration and immersion in this aspect of human behavior created a healthy social balance seems less appealing when it's expressed through the sexual exploitation of two children.

Sure it might be catalyst for creativity, and an integral part of who were are. But if I were having a conversation with Nietzsche today, I might ask him to tag along on a vice raid. He might learn something.

Like the lesson that murky depths of our Dionysian psyche is more intriguing in theory than in practice.

CHAPTER SEVEN:
THE DOPE SANDWICH

As I already mentioned in the first chapter, the debate over policing in this country is as heated as ever. The perception that police are racially insensitive, incompetent, and poorly trained has contributed to a lack of trust between civilians and the officers who serve them.

Truthfully, I think all these viewpoints have some validity, but not for the reasons you might think.

In Baltimore, we send white rookie cops from rural locales into African-American neighborhoods with scant understanding of the people they serve. We train them with military tactics that predispose them to use force too liberally. We teach them little about the law and how to apply it properly. And we deploy more and more officers into tactical units that are completely estranged from the nuance and art of basic police work.

All of this wrong-headed strategy culminates in a department that can t perform the most basic tasks of law enforcement, like investigations and neighborhood problem-solving.

But even the litany of above miscues doesn t fully explain the crisis which afflicts policing today. In fact, one of the primary reasons protesters flood the streets and cops are under siege comes down to simple and essential concept which has long been ignored: accountability.

That is, for years police agencies–including the Baltimore Police Department–have done a miserable job of taking officers to task for wrongdoing. We have not adequately and firmly disciplined cops when they misbehave. We have become too insular and too protective of our own. We have turned into the 'High Priests' Annabelle Sciorra described in the 1997 movie Copland, the tale of a cabal of New York City police officers who thought they were above the law, and to prove it shepherded drugs through a Queens precinct in exchange for low-interest mortgages from the mafia.

The truth is the question of how effectively we hold officers accountable has only recently garnered the attention it deserves, which is why I think it s a concept that is so poorly understood. The recent report released by the Department of Justice on the Baltimore City Police Department revealed a highly dysfunctional internal affairs section that didn t complete investigations and often actively suppressed complaints. It recounted an organization beset with lax procedures and faulty internal investigations that allowed officers to commit acts of wrongdoing with impunity. A bureaucracy so waylaid with conflicts of interest that it couldn t properly investigate officers who broke the law, let alone violate administrative rules.

But I didn t need to read the report to know the BPD s internal affairs unit was a mess.

In 2011 a city cop was busted for dealing heroin from the Northeast District headquarters parking lot. He apparently would coordinate with dealers from his car while standing not too far from a supposed nexus of law enforcement. In fact, federal agents observed him taking delivery of 40 grams of heroin while in uniform standing just a few feet from the district headquarters entrance. It was a brazen, contemptuous crime that totally baffles any sense of probity or ethics for not just him, but the officers he served with.

But what most troubled me about the case were not the allegations of a drug-dealing cop. Instead, I was personally disheartened that it was federal law enforcement, not the BPD, who busted him. In fact, many recent cases of police misconduct prior to the death of Freddie Gray and the indictment of six officers by State's Attorney Marilyn Mosby were prosecuted by our local United States Attorney's office.

In 2010 more than a dozen Baltimore officers were indicted and convicted for their role in a scheme to refer accident victims to a local towing service. The case ensnared cops accepting bribes to ensure that the company not only got lucrative calls for accident tows but repair work as well. The investigation was prompted by a tip from a competing towing firm.

But it is telling that the owner who blew the whistle called the feds, not our internal affairs.

Internal Affairs might seem like a backwater department necessary only for the most egregious cases of police misconduct. But as one of the first internal investigators for the BPD, I can tell you that assumption is decidedly untrue. Nothing is more indicative of a department's overall competence than its integrity. You can't police a community if you can't police yourselves. And you can't solve crimes by committing them.

Believe it or not, maintaining the general honesty of a police department generally dictates how effectively it fights crime.

In part, this equivalence between integrity and effectiveness has much to do with properly regulating the power of the badge and the state of mind it engenders.

To detain, arrest, and otherwise impede a human being is an immense power. The discretion to take away the precious gift of personal freedom dictates the need for tenacious and comprehensive oversight.

For me making an arrest was an occasionally unpleasant task required to enforce the law. No one truthfully does or should enjoy it. And everyone who has had to do it rarely relishes the task.

There are exceptions of course, particularly when the suspect is a hardened or violent criminal who has wreaked havoc on your community, or a cold-blooded murderer who would kill again given the opportunity. But in general, arrests have serious consequences for the person detained, which is why it should be done with precision and thoughtfulness.

But for some, who I believe are poorly trained or ill-equipped to become police, the power to detain can become intoxicating. Handcuffs as a means to settle scores, reprisal for personal slights, and the redress for a bruised ego or low self-esteem. Particularly in a city like Baltimore where arrests were as commonplace as parking tickets, the culture of policing fueled by the imperative to detain as many people as possible has been transformed the process from an act of professionalism and poise to an exercise in brute aggression and naked power.

But this culture of indiscriminate arrests did not evolve overnight. It was allowed to grow and fester due to the department's inability to police itself. Case in point, the cop dealing drugs out of the Northeast District. As the investigation unfolded, we learned he was friends with the head of Internal Investigations. The duo were Facebook buddies, depicted in pictures together on local evening newscasts. I'm not saying it was proof or evidence that anyone looked the other way. But their alleged relationship certainly didn t affirm the functionality or impartiality of the department's internal affairs division, which is why the job of investigating cops is a task which requires an officer who possesses a unique set of skills. It necessitates a detective with excellent investigative instincts capable of dealing with cops who know the tricks of the trade. But you also need an officer with nerves of steel and unmatched integrity who can withstand the unrelenting pressure to look the other way. A delicate balance between technique and operational street smarts I certainly tried to hone during my career.

And perhaps because I worked so hard to learn theses skills I was assigned multiple internal investigations in what was then an ad hoc department. When a cop went astray, I was more often than not asked to investigate.

As a result, I sent several cops to jail throughout my career. Not that I took any pleasure in that, but as I already stated, if you picture a police department akin to a body, then its heart has to beat with integrity. Otherwise, nothing else will operate as it should. You can t stop, solve, and prosecute crimes. Instead, your department becomes a criminal organization with an exceptionally beneficial perk: immunity from the law.

And I speak from experience, because I, too, had to investigate a drug dealing cop. And I also had to execute an elaborate sting and an arrest of a crooked officer working for a department not known for taking down its own. An investigation that occurred during a full-blown and contentious cop strike. And if that wasn t dicey enough, I also had to work not within the sprawling internal affairs department that exists today staffed with dozens of officers, but basically on my own. Just a few of my regular plainclothes officers and me. A notebook, an informant, and a judge willing to sign my warrant.

And like many of my cases involving officers, my investigation didn t start with a tip from a fellow cop. Instead, it came from a criminal informant. Another small-time drug dealer who fed me information. And who asked me a question that stunned me to such a degree at the time, I still remember it liked it happened yesterday.

The query arose during one of my regular check-ins with the CI. Meet-ups with my sources I would schedule periodically to keep up to date on the drug trade in my sector. I would pick him up, drive around in an unmarked car and talk to him. During the ride, he would feed me the latest intelligence on who was dealing what and to whom. Shortly after he got into the vehicle, he asked the question that I still consider one of the most baffling I ve ever heard.

"When did you guys start selling dope?"

"What are you talking about?" I replied, not sure what he meant.

"You guys are selling dope, everyone's talking about it."

"Where?" I asked, incredulous.

"At the district, man. Thats why everyone's talking about it."

"Not possible," I responded. "Couldn't happen."

"Ok, man, suit yourself. But I m telling you there's a cop dealing dope right under your nose."

I didn't interrupt.

"And the funny thing. He'll sell you a sandwich and a kit."

For a moment I had to allow his story to sink in. I'm not naive. I'd already busted a couple errant cops involved in gambling and even sex crimes. But dealing drugs out of a district headquarters just seemed implausible.

"District headquarters, really?" I shot back. "Thats not possible."

"Believe it, man," he replied. "In fact, I can prove it. I can call him right now and set up a buy."

It was a bold offer, but I still had doubts.

"Okay, I'll bite, who?"

"You aren't going to believe it."

"Try me."

The informant paused. "I'm telling you, it's wild."

Before I reveal who he implicated, let me share some insight on informants. They play a controversial yet vital role in policing. They can be excellent sources of information but also dangerously misleading. They can help you make a case or lead you down an interminable path of deception and double-dealing. They are an investigative tool that should be used with caution, skepticism, and suspicion.

And there are several prototypical informants I encountered during my career. Some who exaggerate, some who reluctantly hand over tidbits of varying usefulness. And then there was this guy.

He was always telling tales based upon granular bits of truth. A mercurial character who had a flair for the dramatic. But now he was offering to hand over a case that, if true, was damning. I mean, a cop dealing drugs in district headquarters? An officer of the law doling out narcotics in a bastion of law enforcement? I couldn't help but be both apprehensive and curious about the details he was sharing.

Still, I had doubts. Like I said, most of the cops I had busted to date were involved in illegal gambling, not drug dealing. And if indeed there was a drug-dealing cop it seemed highly unlikely he would be selling retail narcotics out of the Western district, especially since his business was apparently so brazen a small time informant would know all about it. I mean, how was he pulling this off? How on earth could this cop service a bunch of local addicts without a fellow officer noticing? It seemed on the surface implausible.

Still, I couldn't just ignore my informant. What if he was telling the truth? And what if the unthinkable was occurring? That inside a precinct full of sworn law enforcement officers a cop was profiting off the scourge of illicit drugs? It was a potentially perilous crime I had to pursue. True or not I had to follow up, if for no other reason than to ensure I took the allegations seriously and pursued them to the bitter end.

So I plied him for more details. And boy, were they juicy.

First, he said the seller was not a beat cop, but an officer we used to call a turnkey. It's not a term used today, but back then turnkeys were an essential part of district operations. That's because they ran the district headquarter jails.

Today if you drive down Baltimore's main highway known as the Jones Falls Expressway, a monolithic beige building will appear adjacent to the road as you near downtown. It looks like a massive sarcophagus or a mysterious monument to an alien species.

But in fact, its a jail called Central Booking. A facility erected in the 2000s built to process 40,000 prisoners a year. A building that played a critical role in Baltimore's penchant for mass arrests during its horrible experiment with zero tolerance, an era of out-of-control policing I have written about extensively during which the city police department managed to detain 100,000 people annually for nearly six years.

But before the city centralized its jail system (which in fact is controlled by the state), a majority of arrests were processed in the district where they occurred. That means each district had its own jail and courtroom. And of course, a turnkey who was responsible for locking prisoners down and subsequently releasing them from their cells.

It was an important job in what I believe was a more efficient and humane system. We took care of our problems in the community. And as a result, I dont think a ridiculously destructive strategy like zero tolerance could have been implemented even if the politicians wanted it. We just didnt have the capacity.

So as I said, the turnkey was an essential part of district operations. And if it was true he was dealing dope, we were in trouble.

"A pretty cool set-up," my informant continued. "He gives you the dope, the kit, inside a sandwich."

"A sandwich?"

"Yes, its like a one-stop shop."

"And he sells this to prisoners?"

"People locked up, people in the neighborhood. All buyers welcome."

It was information I had trouble comprehending. How in the hell could someone in such a critical role situated in the heart of headquarters sell heroin inside a sandwich? And how on earth could he be perpetrating this crime in broad daylight within full view of a building full of cops?

"Are you sure?" I asked again.

"Like I said, let s call him."

Of course, like all dicey cases—and believe me, investigating a cop is dicey—it didn t occur in a vacuum. In fact, the drama that was unfolding with the drug peddling turnkey was happening at the same time the city police department was in the midst of a highly contentious strike.

In 1974 over 400 cops walked off the job, upset about low pay and benefits. Commissioner Donald Pomerleau had fired all of them, asserting police officers were public servants who couldn t just decide not to show up for work. His argument: the strike was illegal.

The strike was eventually called off after Pomerleau agreed to give officers better benefits and more flexible work rules. Most of the officers were re-hired. But it was a tense atmosphere in which to conduct an independent internal affairs investigation.

So I was pretty much on my own. I had to tread carefully to make the sure the case was airtight. And critical to that goal was using detectives I could trust. We all had to keep their mouths shut to ensure the probe didn t leak out. After all, it would take only one set of loose lips to tip off the turnkey and turn the whole investigation into an exercise in futility,

Thus I initially kept my CI s allegations to myself. I didn t tell anyone about my suspicions during the preliminary investigation. I arranged for the informant to make a call from his house. I would listen on the other line, take notes, and go from there.

No one else would know.

The night of the call my informant was ebullient. I guess getting a cop in trouble was a sort of poetic justice for a guy who had a fairly long rap sheet.

When he picked up the phone and dialed, I have to admit I was hoping the call wouldn't pan out. Like I said, I didn't relish putting anyone behind bars, even a cop. But if he was dealing drugs from the district and profiting from it while fellow officers were risking their lives to take the same drugs off the street, it was a case where I wouldn t have a problem putting the handcuffs on myself. I always felt a sense of betrayal when a cop wearing the same badge I did violated his or her oath. It reflected poorly on all of us and played into the stereotype of crooked cops working both sides of the drug war.

Bear in mind, as stupid and excessive as the war against illicit narcotics has become, back then it was different. Most of us viewed it as a last ditch effort to preserve the dignity of our community. Selling dope was no joke. It spread addiction like a virus through the neighborhoods already economically strung out by the force of deindustrialization. I don t agree with the method or the madness of the drug warrior mentality now, but during the 1970s it felt like we were trying to turn back a tide of human misery which was slowly drowning the city in a flood of despair and disillusionment.

So I was hoping that the tip turned out to be a red herring. Just a fatuous tale from an informant looking to sully a good cop. But those hopes were soon dashed. The phone call went just as my informant promised. It was like ordering a take-out pizza or sorting through value menu options at a drive through window.

"What do you need?" the turnkey asked.

"A bag, and a kit," my informant responded.

"Be here in twenty."

"Oh, and you got a sandwich, right?"

"Right between the bread," he replied.

And that was it. He hung up the phone, shot me a glance, and practically jumped out of his chair. "Let s do this!"

"Not so fast, we need to plan this out. For now, stay put and keep your mouth shut."

His disappointment was palpable. He wanted us to charge into Western

District headquarters and make an arrest. But I knew we had to be cautious. If we didn t follow procedure, conduct this investigation by the book, it would be over before it started.

Bear in mind, if you think cops don t like internal affairs now, you can only imagine the animosity toward us more that forty years ago. Stirring the pot was the strike. It was contentious, public, and fluid. And I wasn t sure if arresting a dope-dealing officer would be perceived as retribution. A poorly timed probe aimed at tarnishing the reputation of the rank-and-file.

I was also a bit unsure of how to proceed. I wasn t confident that instructing my informant to walk into district headquarters was the best way to build a case. Sure he might be able to make a buy, but we didn t have the type of sophisticated video equipment we have now. So if he executed a hand-to-hand purchase, the case could turn into a cop's word against a small-time drug dealer. A guy with a mile long rap sheet and an improbable story about buying drugs and sandwich from a turnkey deep inside district headquarters. Not the best strategy to net a successful prosecution.

So I decided to focus on the stash. The place where the crooked cop was hiding the drugs between sales. I know it sounds counterintuitive, but if we could find out where he was storing the narcotics, the rest of the case would be easier to build.

That's the beauty and the pitfall of drug laws. If a suspect has a specific quantity in his or her possession, I don't have to prove intent. The amount does the work in the eyes of the law. I'm not sure if I m comfortable with that concept in general, but it certainly made it easy—perhaps too easy—to build a case.

So we worked the investigation through our informant. He did, in fact, make a buy. We staked out the district and watched him walk in with the cash and exit with a bag of dope, a needle, and a ham sandwich. It was distressing, to say the least.

Especially because the turnkey was working what s known as the midnight shift–from midnight to 8:00 a.m. the next day. It was a period of time that was often busy with arrests, particularly over the weekend, but often lightly staffed. Which is why I wasn't totally astonished as we witnessed him exit headquarters several times during the shift and retrieve something from his car parked in the district headquarters lot. We couldn't be totally sure, but it certainly seemed logical he stored the illicit wares in the auto.

Either way, we had enough to get a warrant. I wrote it out and brought to a judge who signed it, but gave me a quizzical look in the process.

"Dealing out of the district, Steve?"

"I'm afraid so, sir," was all I could manage.

The next evening we showed up at headquarters with the warrant to the search the car. I presented it to the turnkey who turned fifty shades of pale when I handed him the piece of paper. For a second he just stood there and gaped, apparently utterly surprised that his scheme was exposed. When he opened his mouth, I interrupted him.

"I wouldn't say anything if I were you," I advised him. "You have the right to remain silent, and of course anything you say now could used against you in court. So I think you should keep your mouth shut."

Apparently heeding my advice, he sat down at his desk and slumped in his chair.

Inside the car, we found quite an assortment of drugs. Heroin, marijuana, and cocaine. We confiscated a scale, baggies, and all the requisite paraphernalia of a full-time drug dealer. It was a bountiful haul of narcotics. There was also two loaves of white Wonder Bread and an assortment of deli meats, ham, bologna, and pastrami. Basically, the Western District had become a makeshift pharmacy and incidental sandwich shop for the entire neighborhood.

After the search, we made the arrest. As I expressed at the beginning of the chapter, no one likes to haul someone off in handcuffs; its just part of the job. But in this case, I felt less ambivalent. I was a constant witness to the deadly wake of destruction caused by illicit drugs in my city. I watched neighborhoods in my district transformed from stable blue-collar communities to crime-infested war zones. I had seen addiction tear families apart and put children out onto the street. And I had participated in the increasingly aggressive drug war which I thought then and still believe transformed policing from a civilian profession into a quasi-military job.

So I took some pleasure in slapping cuffs on this perpetrator. I took even more pleasure watching my informant testify at his trial. And I felt completely satisfied when the judge handed down an eight-year sentence, sternly upbraiding the officer for betraying the badge and his oath.

And you know what, for all the misdeeds top brass and politicians cover up out of fear of bad publicity, this case had the opposite effect. The public didn't perceive it as just another example of a corrupt cop. Instead, the prosecution was welcomed as an example of the department finally starting to get a handle on internal corruption. We got credit for rooting it out, and following through with a conviction. It was a case that demonstrated we meant business about integrity, and probably a good workplace prophylactic for cops contemplating using the badge for personal gain and criminal conduct.

In the end, I think there is nothing our profession can accomplish that is more important towards improving police and community relations than to prosecute cops who forget wearing a badge also means taking an oath to uphold the law. Only in doing so we will we rebuild trust.

Only by removing lawbreakers from the profession will that trust be warranted, which is why I think we have to make this case when we debate the state of policing in America. Without a system of accountability, reliable internal affairs investigators, and some sense among officers that screwing up will be met with fair and firm discipline, you really can't judge just how good or bad a department is. Police need guidelines, and they must be trained to follow them. Sometimes that means you have to lock them up. It's not an easy task, but essential if we want competent and effective law enforcement in a country that truly needs it.

CHAPTER EIGHT:
A FAILURE TO COMMUNICATE

There are incidents involving police that often seem inexplicable.

Shootings of unarmed men that consume the country in a fierce debate about law enforcement tactics. Seemingly brutal arrests that cannot be explained solely by circumstance. Routine traffic stops that end with guns drawn and suspects dead. In short, a variety of actions and behavior which to the untrained eye seem wholly odd and utterly bizarre.

But I can explain it. All of it. And without the usual rationalizations and patronizing garbage which pervades the debates over how a community should be policed. I can explain much of it without resorting to the typical cop talk that you don't know what it's like to make a life or death split second decision. Or only a cop can judge a cop.

While it is true policing, like all occupations, has its own particular perspective, the idea that community standards and common sense should be entirely excluded from the process of judging how and why we do our jobs is just foolish. When your profession involves the absolute and irrevocable act of taking a life, excluding the people who empower you to make such a profound decision is untenable. Put simply, if we're going to shoot and kill people, we have to have to justify it with more than a shrug and callow proffering that you just can't understand why we did it.

As a man who has taken a life, I should know. Yes, it is a singularly horrifying and terrifying experience that I recounted in detail in my first book, You Cant Stop Murder. But as the inventor of contemporary policing Sir Robert Peele, who I discussed in the first chapter, stipulated, it's an act that should be explicable. The decision to use deadly force should and must conform to the standards of the community it affects. To argue that somehow it's just an internal matter outside the purview of public dialog seems alarmingly Kafkaesque.

And yet that appears to be precisely the type of justification offered in defense of many controversial police-involved shootings or inexplicable arrests. Too often we, and I mean police, try to defend the indefensible with stonewalling and silence. It's not morally right, and it only makes matters worse.

But how did we get here? And why does policing as an institution seem to be moving farther away from the community, not closer? And why does hardly a week pass when a new debate emerges over a disturbing video of a violent encounter with cops that the thrusts both sides further apart?

I think much of this disconnect can be explained in very brief conversation I had with a cadet at the Baltimore police academy almost a decade ago. A short exchange that typifies the wrong-headed philosophy that pervades policing today.

He had completed roughly half his training program. A hard-working young man imbued with the type of enthusiasm that keeps us old folks hopeful about the future of our profession. But there was just one problem. He wasn t trained to be a cop.

How do I know?

Based upon a few fateful words uttered by him shortly after the conclusion of my class on policing and the constitution. I asked him how his training was going.

"Well, sir, I earned a near perfect score on the target range and placed third in physical training."

"Well thats good," I replied. "But what does that have to do with policing?"

The cadet looked baffled. "I dont understand?"

"Do you know how to testify in court and win a conviction?" I asked.

"Well, not yet. But thats not how I m evaluated. Why would that matter?"

And that was it: the answer, which offered the presentment of what ails policing today. Young and impressionable cops being prepared to work the streets like soldiers. Training for what they call 'action,' not law enforcement. A mentality cultivated by the culture in our law enforcement educational system that I've often said feels more like a military boot camp than a police academy. In fact, at our police academy, they call the first week of training as "boot camp." You get the idea.

So when the next controversy emerges over an allegedly trigger-happy cop, or police are caught on video manhandling a suspect, keep this in mind: they are literally following their training.

It might seem hard to believe we don't teach all police officers how to negotiate, navigate or otherwise approach the job with any subtlety. But we don't and have not, particularly in Baltimore. Here we emphasize action and aggression, takedowns and marksmanship. Skills that are more suitable for a battlefield.

And there is more lost in this emphasis on physicality than a nuanced understanding of the law. A more pronounced lack of truly understanding law enforcement than the omission of a few techniques like de-escalation training. There is something quintessential to the art of policing that evaporates into the aether of military-style SWAT teams and assault rifle-bearing.

That's because our job at its most basic is to maintain a civil society, not assault it. What we do, and how we succeed, require a more subtle and psychological skill set than the cadet who has been taught to shoot and fight. The ability to communicate with people and de-escalate tensions that derive from understanding not just how that process works, but why. What do I mean? Think about it: our ultimate job as cops is not to jump out of cars or stop and frisk random motorists. That's only the beginning.

The final arbiter of our work is the courtroom. In other words, the process of law enforcement was designed to facilitate the adjudication of the law. And it is in the courtroom where we must excel to achieve that goal. If we can't investigate, interrogate, and testify to obtain convictions, then we can't function as law enforcers. And if we're not training officers to enforce the law in court, what exactly do we want them to do?

Well, I think we know. And I think as a nation we have witnessed what this emphasis on aggressive training has wrought.

Learning to investigate, testify, and ultimately articulate the law is more than just an ancillary training issue. It's a process that develops the most productive, albeit underutilized, skill an officer can learn. A professional proficiency fundamental to good policing: communication.

That's right: being able to talk to someone, to persuade, to cajole. It is one of the most useful techniques a cop can master; a skill set that all starts with the ability to converse. It's a tactic useful in a million different capacities. Testifying, interrogation, stop and frisk, working sources, or even crowd control But more importantly a technique that can potentially avert many of the most troubling types of policing we witness today.

Of course, I'm not talking about the gift of gab possessed by a car salesman. Or the flowing rhetorical whimsy that occasionally infects politicians. What I'm focused upon is the strategic use of verbal interactions to advance a case by drawing out a witness or tripping up a suspect. The ability to converse in a meaningful way that can elicit useful leads, timely confessions, and compelling testimony. It's a complex skill that requires training, a familiarity with the law, and a frank understanding of the community you serve.

But it's an indispensable talent that was always invaluable to me. In fact, one of the most daunting burglary cases I ever worked was pretty much solved solely with effective communication. A rash of crime that came to an end only with a bit of creativity, cunning, and talking. And more importantly, police work that provided a productive outcome without the use of a gun, baton, or even a crime lab. And it was the type of case that rarely gets solved, much to the detriment of the community.

In Baltimore, murders and violence make headlines. Shootings and carjackings draw the focus of a large part of the city's law enforcement resources. But anyone who lives here will tell you that crimes like burglary and larceny affect a larger swathe of the city's population.

Yes, murder is heinous and street robberies are terrifying, but its more likely that a resident will be victimized by the hundreds of property crimes that occur daily. And the sad fact is, these types of personal violations are rarely solved. In fact, I was always of the opinion that it wasnt drug dealing or even the high homicide rate that depleted the citys population, but the continual drumbeat of petty thievery. Stolen lawn equipment and household break-ins, car thefts, and property crimes that in part accelerated the departure of the citys dwindling population base.

Property crime was a particular concern of mine when I became a plainclothes officer in the city's Central District. The Central was home to the city's most densely populated business community. It was also adjacent to wealthy neighborhoods like Guildford and Homeland just north of downtown. All of these areas taken together comprised one of the city's most targeted locales for thieves.

With warehouses, massive departments stores like Hutzler's and Macys, and an active and busy port, the opportunity for an enterprising criminal is nearly limitless. Add to that a cornucopia of ornate row homes and even more impressive estates just a few miles north, and the entire swath of the city was a burglars paradise.

Which is why I was nearly always enmeshed in some sort of theft case.

Chapter Eight: A Failure to Communicate   **115**

The calls were endless. The crimes were unrelenting. It seemed at times like the city's small remainders of wealth was like a picnic left outside to be picked over by the population that was increasing sliding into poverty. You just couldn't keep anything safe from a growing populace seemingly determined to steal it.

And just like the city's continuum of violence, the crimes tended to come in waves. Which is exactly how one of the worst examples of concerted thievery I ever investigated began. A string of burglaries that we couldn't solve. That is, until a beat cop had a conversation with a suspect.

As I've said over and over, the uniformed officer on the streets is the lifeblood of any department. They are the first on the scene of a murder and the last to leave when the yellow tape is rolled up. They possess the most knowledge about the community in which they work. If I needed leads to identify a suspect or to locate a person of interest in a sector, it was the patrol officer who I asked first. And that's where this case started: a uniformed officer doing his job and doing it well.

It was the summer of 1968, and we had a big problem. A serial burglar was hitting homes in several downtown communities with alarming regularity. The crimes were exacting and numerous, stretching from the hip Mt. Vernon midtown neighborhood and as far north as Homeland. If you aren't familiar with the city, Mt. Vernon is a fashionable hipster haunt replete with towering brownstones and trendy restaurants. Homeland is one of the city's priciest communities, dotted with sprawling estates and palatial homes built by the 19th-century merchants and the shipping magnates who made Baltimore the country's third wealthiest city in the country by the 1850s.

The heists were occurring at a rapid clip. Several dozen burglaries were netting scores of electronics, jewelry, cash, and other valuables. The perpetrators were smart. They apparently knew how to bypass home alarm systems. They only struck when the homeowners were out. They seemed to move efficiently through their targets without leaving a single fingerprint or clue of any kind.

But it was the similarity of the crimes that kept me up at night. Patterns revealed in the aftermath of each incident that revealed just how effective this group of criminals could be.

A sloppy burglar generally leaves a mess that is easy to decipher: broken glass, a tripped alarm, and fingerprints. Poorly organized thieves leave clues that help solve a case quickly. Amateurs are easier to catch, and more likely to make mistakes that lead to arrest.

But whoever was committing these crimes was a pro. He or she barely left a dresser drawer open or a closet door ajar. They would hit their targets quickly and be gone in minutes. Again, they knew how to bypass alarm systems and seem to have a pretty good idea of how to pick a lock and jimmy a window with the least amount of damage. And the geographical spread of targets was varied enough to make it hard to figure out where they would strike next. All told, we counted roughly three-dozen burglaries that fit this pattern. It was, quite frankly, an unholy mess.

But as I said before, when in doubt, communicate.

So my first step towards implementing an effective communication strategy began by disseminating the critical details of the burglaries to all patrol officers across the city. We asked supervisors to read them at roll call daily. And it didn't take long for the strategy to produce results.

A Central District patrol officer, one of the unheralded rank-and-file, was patrolling an alley after he heard what he thought was the sound of breaking glass. To his surprise, halfway in he encountered a boy just 14 years old carrying a rather large television set. The boy barely flinched when the officer told him to stop.

He asked him where he got it. The boy seemed nonplussed, the officer recounted later.

"He told me there was an apartment that was full of TVs," the officer recounted, "and other stuff as well. He said it was no big deal he took it because they had plenty to spare."

And here's the first step in the so-called chain of communication that ultimately led to solving the crime. Not just a lesson in good talking but why a strategic approach to communicating can be a critical step in solving a case. How a decision to talk and gather information rather than just make an arrest can potentially lead to a more productive outcome.

The officer could have grabbed the bounty and handcuffed the boy. But instead, as he related to me, this particular officer decided to take a more pragmatic approach.

"I said I was impressed, and can you show me this place?"

And the boy indeed compiled, leading the officer to the door of an apartment building right around the corner. Inside he promptly showed the officer the number of the abode where he found the television set. Of course, the officer couldn't just walk into the alleged stash house. He needed a warrant. Which is when he contacted me.

So I wrote a warrant detailing the encounter between the police and the boy. A warrant that a judge quickly approved. With two detectives in tow, we visited the apartment where the boy told the officer he procured his prize television. There was no one home when we arrived, so the landlord let us in. And wow, what a stash we discovered.

It was like a Best Buy superstore on steroids. Television sets piled sky high. Phonographs and 8-track tape players stacked to the ceiling. Jewelry boxes and knickknacks sorted neatly into perfectly aligned rows. There was even an extensive collection of records and 8-track cartridges boxed and alphabetized.

It was a cornucopia of electronics and valuables. A take so extensive the stash house seemed like a potential entry into the unofficial BPD record books. Apparently the burglar applied the same exacting sense of precision and care to storing the goods as they did stealing them. I was frankly dumbfounded by the scope of it all.

But at least we had a lead.

So we obtained the name of the person who leased the apartment. I assigned two detectives to wait for her, not him, to return. In fact, I was a little surprised that the person of interest whose name appeared on the document was female.

Not to sound sexist, but women commit far fewer crimes than men. Particularly premeditated crimes like burglaries. And forget violence, even rarer still. So I was curious, to say the least, about the suspect who was more than likely behind this up until now highly effective operation.

My detectives staked out the abode. They waited patiently for nearly 12 hours. Finally, after half a dozen cups of coffee, the tenant returned. My officers detained her, and she was quickly transported to Central District headquarters for questioning. To be honest, when I work a case like this, I expect to arrest someone I'm familiar with. A career criminal with all the personal habits of an experienced thief. But what I encountered inside the interrogation room confounded all those expectations. For one thing, as I already stated, it was a her. A small, stout women with slicked back hair dressed in pressed shirt and slacks.

Her gaze was unflinching. Her energy coiled into a straight-backed posture. And most telling of all, her natural poise indicated to me she was nonplussed. Meaning she appeared unfazed sitting across a table from a BPD detective. That explaining how she obtained an apartment full of electronics was a nuisance, not a dilemma.

I started this chapter arguing that good communication is critical to good policing, and how learning the nuances of effective talking is an essential skill if you want to solve crimes. And so I began my interrogation with the one essential element that is a critical part of this artful discipline: a strategy. Or better put, observing and listening to the person who is sitting across the table from you to discern an approach to talking to them.

My take on her was simple. She was not a perp who would break under direct questioning. She looked prepared for it. Tough and resolved, not compliant or scared. So hounding her about the burglaries or the stash in her apartment would probably net little. In fact, it might even elicit a call to a lawyer. I had to take a different approach. I had to appeal to a different aspect of personality. I had to appeal to her ego. That may seem like a silly way to question an apparently compulsive thief, but think about it for a minute.

She was obviously good at her job. Given the immaculately organized haul we discovered in her apartment and the consistent pattern of meticulous—almost untraceable—crimes, it seemed fairly obvious this was a skill set she had honed with some effort. So instead of making her confess, which would be almost certainly contentious, I figured why not try to get her talking about herself? Remember the famous biblical phrase, 'Pride goeth before a fall?'

Well, take it from a cop, it's true.

Now I can imagine you might be thinking, why the hell appeal to the pride of a criminal? Why coddle a person who had wreaked havoc on the sanctity of the homes of dozens of families? Why even waste time assuaging her ego when all you have to do is get her to explain what the hell she was doing living in an apartment full of turntables and boom boxes?

There are two simple answers. Remember, I said at the beginning the job of a cop is to get a conviction in court. Well, that's precisely what I was thinking. The more a suspect talks, the easier it becomes to make the case. The more they're willing to open up, the more likely they will say something incriminating. And if she were the personality type I suspected, a good conversation would be a more effective strategy than an unrelenting grilling.

The other fact worth mentioning is that the legal system is based upon logic, not vengeance. In other words, the entire point of the process of law enforcement is to stop crime. Therefore, my job was to connect as many dots as possible. To find out just how extensive her involvement was and how many homes she had hit. And also to learn if she had accomplices. And ultimately, to charge her to the fullest extent possible for the crimes she had committed.

One other aspect of criminal interrogation worth noting is that a suspect has the absolute right to end it anytime without cause or reason. The right to remain silent is an integral part of the constitution, and I deeply respect it. If she decided at any moment that she didn't want to talk, our conversation was over.

After that, the case would be constructed with forensics, fingerprints and serial numbers. A much more painstaking process, and often subject to false positives and courtroom challenges.

Which is why took a leisurely approach. I just started talking, about anything; a conversation that was both wide-ranging and fluid. Her likes and dislikes. Her taste in music. And as we conversed she loosened up a bit. So when I thought she was totally relaxed, I appealed to her ego.

"I have to be honest, you know quite a bit about a lot of things," I said. She didn't answer but smiled. "So I'm just wondering, I'm curious. I've been investigating burglaries all my career, and I've never seen anything like what we found in your apartment. That was quite a haul.

"The thing is, I don't see how anyone pulls something like that off. I mean, that must have been quite an operation. How many houses did you hit? Do you even remember?" I continued.

"I mean, at this point we got the entire haul in your apartment, so you're already tied to the crimes. But what I really want to know, is how the hell did you do it?"

Now, you might think this was too obvious a ploy to work. Or that this apparently smart burglar would be too savvy to answer a pitifully leading question. But as I pointed out in the previous chapter, if there is one singular and universal truism I've learned being a cop, is that the ego overwhelms the rational thought process. That is our penchant for self-aggrandizement negates even our deepest instinct for self-preservation. We are, as people, almost pathological in our need to stand out. Which is why her answer didn't come as a total surprise.

"Do you want me to show you?"

"Show me?" I asked, just to make sure I understood.

"I can show you all of them, I remember all the details," she replied, adding, "Can we drive?"

I fumbled for a moment, a bit surprised my gambit was working. "We can drive wherever you want."

And so I quickly procured a car from the district, and we went for a drive. Me, the eager detective, and the city's best thief sitting in a car taking a driving tour of the most profound string of burglaries I'd ever investigated. It was, to say the least, an enlightening excursion.

She guided me from home to home, neighborhood to neighborhood past each of the locations she had burglarized. It was like a hit parade of the city's best break-ins.

Amazingly, at each stop, she would recall intimate details about the house. The exact location of a bedroom closet. The hidden crawlspace that contained a treasure trove of jewelry. The manufacturer's brand of the alarm system and how to override it. It was an embarrassment of investigative riches. All I did was listen and take notes. And all she did was talk. In the end, she gave up the details of not a dozen, but roughly 61 cases. Along with the breathtaking scope of break-ins, she told me about her two accomplices as well. By the time she had finished, I had solved the biggest burglary case of my career with little more than good conversation.

It turns out the group behind the crime spree was a gang of sorts. A group of tightly knit lesbians who worked in teams identifying targets, reverse engineering alarms systems and fencing the haul. I was seriously impressed. In the end, all three women affiliated with the gang were convicted. I ended up doing the essential and basic task of being a cop, testifying in court against all of them. Building a strong case from the inside out. And obtaining most of the evidence by simply by talking.

It took some time, but we were able to return a good chunk of the stolen items to their rightful owners. And more importantly, a destructive crime wave that was undermining the safety and security of dozens of residents was shut down. It was an efficient and productive process that lead to precisely the kind of outcome good law enforcement is supposed to produce.

But more important is how this result was achieved. Not through specialized units or armored cars, or with aggressive tactics or zero tolerance arrests. No arm-twisting and coercion. We didn't even need to use pricey technology and obtrusive devices now favored by police agencies nationwide.

We applied an age-old tactic that never seemed to fail me in a bind.

We communicated.

CHAPTER NINE:
HUMAN, ALL TOO HUMAN

Our destiny exercises its influence over us even when, as yet, we have not learned
its nature: it is our future that lays down the law of our today.

Frederick Nietzsche - Human, All Too Human (1878)

We are all human. Too human.

Meaning both cops and civilians. Two sides of the same imperfect coin joined at the hip in a continuing process we call community.

We conjure associations to salve our instinctive need to alleviate uncertainty, danger, and fear. We invent institutions like policing to address these same anxieties. We expect the process of law enforcement to neutralize existential threats, real or imagined. And in doing so we create a public institution–policing–that can sometimes be as unpredictable and unwieldy as the extreme behaviors it is designed to ameliorate.

But this imperfect solution has us in common. It relies on our conflicting human ingenuity and commitment to work. Which means it is as flawed as the people who created it, us.

Think about it: if humans weren't inherently flawed, why would we need cops at all? If people didn't make grievous errors in judgment, why pass laws?

But we forget that people are cops too. Human beings tasked with adjudicating our laws. To stand on the corner and arbitrate aberrant behavior and destructive impulses. Which means all the foibles that make policing necessary are inextricably linked to the people who wear the badge. And we the police forget that the people we serve are also influenced by the same contradictory imperatives of human nature.

In a sense, we both suffer from a similar malady: we are both human, all too human.

I raise the dilemma of our shared humanity because it underlies the essential thrust of this book, The Book of Cop: understanding the complex reality of our conflicted selves. The fickle canvas of being. The bestial nature of the human psyche. The violent strain of our worst impulses we task police to restrain, if not vanquish.

Dealing with the most destructive human tendencies will always be an occupation that entails both danger and unforeseen consequences. I don't think we honestly acknowledge how it affects the people asked to confront it for a living. Or reflect upon exactly what type of commitment completing that task entails from both sides.

Because disorder inflicts pain not just upon a community, but both the men and women asked to contain it. We cannot ignore the consequences of this troubling intersection of human depravity and our desire to free of it. The sometimes toxic mixture of laws and lawbreakers it conjures, and the fallout that results from dealing with it daily.

So we must consider the dichotomous aspects of our conflicted humanity when we debate how and why we police. And that dialog must start with the simple but often overlooked premise: we're only human

This oft-forgotten fact informs the ultimate question of what it means to be a cop. To minimize the adverse effect of aberrant human behavior we must first try to understand it. To put murderers behind bars and take rapists off the streets through civilized means we have to comprehend the complex psychology that drives these abhorrent impulses. To keep the peace when disorder reigns and to restore calm when safety seems elusive we must strive to understand the frustrations and motives of the people who initiate unrest.

It is all of these contradictions I have attempted to wrestle with in The Book of Cop. The divide between our aspirations and deviance, the border between peace and chaos. The different elements of the human psyche which seem incongruent and irreconcilable. A duality that spawns kindness and violence, compassion and murder. A split between or social and anti-social selves which will never be truly be resolved because we cannot escape our human limitations.

Which is why I'm going to end this book with one of the most painful cases of my career. A crime involving a cop who violated his oath and dishonored the badge.

You might wonder, why do I keep recounting the bad behavior of cops? What's the point of writing The Book of Cop if it devolves into a litany of bad police behavior? What exactly are you trying to prove?

Well, part of my argument, that in our debate over policing we leave our humanity at the door, means we have to acknowledge just how human we are. That is, to come clean about our flaws. To explore in detail the mistakes cops make. That we must, once and for all lay bare the worst among us and be upfront and honest about their misdeeds.

But there is another reason for exploring the worst behavior of individual police officers I've encountered. An aspect of the being a cop that often goes unacknowledged. Put simply, wearing a badge and strapping on a gun doesn't change the underlying character of the person. Entering the police academy and sitting through hours of training does not irrevocably alter the nature of an individual. We must acknowledge that before we can collectively come up with better ways to reform the institution of policing, we have to consider what we all have in common.

As you might recall, at the beginning of this book I argued one of the most destructive trends in policing today is the mythologizing of the profession. An overwrought rhetorical effort by politicians and police to construe policing as an occupation replete with unimpeachable practitioners. Well, I suppose one informal way to counteract that trend is to puncture the myth. That is, to tell the truth, to be honest about the best, and worst, of us.

I also want to drive home the point that bad cops can and need to be stopped. And argue that much of this behavior can be prevented if we acknowledge the fundamental inconsistencies of human nature, and most importantly, its intrinsic potential for both bad and good. And better yet, by fully embracing our flaws we can come up with ways to identify, perhaps and remove, the most destructive actors who wear the uniform before they cause harm.

Which is why in this next-to-the-last chapter I again will be telling the story of a bad cop. Consider it a twisted olive branch to the people I continue to serve. If indeed I'm willing to be honest about the worst among us, then perhaps you will also believe me that we can together fix the problems which beset policing today. That we can improve policing, make cops better at their jobs, and quell the distrust that pervades our professionals and the communities they serve. Hell, I'm 87, that means I'm a providential optimist. Believe me, when you're my age simply getting out of bed to debate the future makes you irrepressibly upbeat.

So I can promise this because that's exactly what I did during my tenure at the Baltimore Police Department: I held police accountable.

As I've already shared, I arrested several people who wore the badge. Each officer a pox upon our profession.

But the case I'm about to recount stands out. It was not only one of the most troubling cases of police misconduct and moral transgression I ever investigated, but also taught me was just how important the task of watching cops was. It was a horrible sex crime involving an officer and a teenage girl that was one of the worst examples of cop criminality I have ever witnessed. And what made matters worse, it involved a cop who was well known in the community he served. An officer who feigned a connection to the people, but used that link to commit an unthinkable crime.

The story begins with a father coming home from work. Except when he entered his abode expecting to be greeted by his family he instead was confronted by a bizarre scene: a female friend of his juvenile teenage daughter coming down the stairs, a man following right behind her. But not just any random adult.

A cop.

The father, a resident of South Baltimore, had asked his daughter to babysit her three younger siblings while he worked. She enlisted a 17-year-old neighborhood acquaintance to help. With seemingly adequate care in place, he left his family behind for his job at the now defunct Broening Highway General Motors plant.

But his return, as I said before, involved an awkward if not inexplicable scene. His daughter's friend walking down the stairs disheveled and distraught, and a neighborhood cop named David, well known to him, and others following shortly behind her. It was so strange the father later told me he didn't know what to say.

The cop informed the somewhat flummoxed man that the babysitter had a sinus infection and that he was just 'checking on her.'

"I was a little confused," he told me later. "It didn't look right. But I knew the officer. He was friends with everybody.

"So I believed him."

Any other person walking down the steps might not have made it through the front door. But the badge sometimes earns us a free pass.

The officer departed without saying another word. The young woman, still apparently agitated but also reluctant to talk, returned home. The father told me later while he was unsure of what to do, he felt instinctively something was amiss.

"She just seemed so messed up. Like something pretty bad had happened."

And it didn't take long for that something to be revealed. Shortly after the officer ventured back onto the streets and the young girl returned home, I got a call from a supervisor in the Central District.

"Steve, we have a mother down here in the District who says her daughter was raped."

"Ok," I replied. "Isn't that a sex crime case?"

"She claims it was cop, which is why I was told to call you," he said, adding, "and she's a juvenile."

I hung up the phone. My mind raced. A cop raping a kid? Seriously?

If it were true, it would be a horrific case. An officer of the law abusing a child. A cop who was sworn to protect and serve both the community and the law raping a juvenile? It doesn't get much worse.

When I arrived at district headquarters, I was given a quick briefing on the details of the mother's story. It was ugly, to say the least. Frankly, I didn't want to hear another tale of a cop who had not just abused his badge. But it's part of the job, and as I said before, it was often specifically part of my job.

When I sat down with the mother and her daughter, the child looked terrified. Her eyes were bloodshot and swollen. Her unkempt hair matted to her face like a greasy mask. She leaned her thin frame into her mother's shoulder, shuddering as I opened my notebook and began to write.

Her mother sat stiffly in a chair beside her. One arm draped across her daughter's shoulders, the other outstretched to emphasize her outrage.

"Are you going to arrest this guy?" She asked before I had uttered a word. "I believe so, ma'am, but first I need to hear the story, all of it," I replied. "Every detail, no matter how difficult."

"She's gone through too much," the mother shot back.

"I understand, but without her statement, I don t have a case," I replied. "Just tell me what happened."

And that's what she and her daughter did, recounting to me in a series of chilling descriptions one of the worst cases of a cop gone bad I ever have ever heard.

The day began like any other for the 17-year-old. She was sitting with her friend on a stoop in Southwest Baltimore, watching the youngsters play on the sidewalk. It was a typical balmy summer evening in Baltimore. Neighbors commiserating about the heat, the sultry summer air hanging like an angry cloud over everything.

Then a local beat cop drove up in his patrol car. He beckoned the victim to the driver s side window. She obliged.

"Everybody knows him," she told me. "They say he s a friendly cop." The officer, she said, asked her about a recent incident when she ran away from home. Had she done it again, he queried. "I said no," she recalled. "And then he told me he would be back later and I should fix him some coffee.

"And so I did."

But before he drove away, he said something else, an offhand remark that startled her. "I m going to date you when you turn 18. Right now you re just jailbait."

The victim told me she was shaken a bit. She said there was nothing unusual about David stopping by for coffee, he'd done it before. It was routine for patrol cops to visit the homes in the district where they worked. When I walked the beat, I'd take the occasional breather inside a resident's home. And quite often that included coffee.

But the remark about dating, that was another story. It made her apprehensive. And she said she grew tense waiting for him to return.

About an hour later David showed up. He entered the row home and strode to the kitchen. Without saying anything he starting drinking the coffee. Halfway through the cup, he received a radio call. And that's where things turned bizarre.

He told the teen he would be back in an hour. But as he walked to the door, he put his arm around her. That's right, a grown man and officer of the law draping his arm around a teenage girl inside a row home. All of it occurring as her young friend sat on the couch. It was beyond brazen, but he didn't stop there. Suddenly he turned her around and grabbed her by both shoulders. "He kissed me," she said, her eyes filling with tears. "He kissed me on the mouth."

It was for her, as she described it, nauseating. As she disclosed the intimate details of how the cop forced his tongue into her mouth I, too, was sickened. As I said before, I have three daughters of my own. And the thought of any man, no less a cop, violating any one of them conjured a similar reaction in my gut: nausea.

But that was just the beginning.

When David returned, the victim was lying on the couch. She told me his violent and unexpected kiss made her feel ill. She hoped being laid out and visibly distraught would discourage further advances. But that was not the case.

In fact, his behavior got worse.

"He told me to go upstairs to the bedroom," she recounted.

She felt trapped, isolated. She repeated over and over again that he was a police officer. A man she trusted. But her anxiety was only heightened by the fact that he wore the badge, which meant in her mind she had nowhere to turn. When she told him she felt sick he again suggested moving to an upstairs bedroom.

"You need to cool off," he said, noting the room had an air conditioner. "You have heat exhaustion."

But the victim didn't want to move. She pleaded with him to leave her alone. But he was insistent. Finally, he simply picked her up by her waist and carried her up into the bedroom, laid her on the bed, and slammed the door behind him. It was stunning. Like some sort of hunter, he had simply hoisted his prey, slung it over his shoulder, and claimed it as his own. An unconscionable act performed in front of a cadre of children who I can only imagine must have been confused at the very least. But as bad as that was, things got so ugly when he carried her into the bedroom I feel uncomfortable telling the rest of the story.

He dropped her on the bed. She tried to get under the covers and hide. But he wasn't having it, ripping off her shoes and grappling with her as she struggled to break free. Then he yanked off her bra and pulled down her pants.

She protested. But he didn't stop.

Before I continue, I want to make a point about sex crimes and rape in general that I think few men understand. I have investigated enough of these terrible crimes to share some insight on how the victims feel.

Men, by and large, outweigh women and have uniformly superior strength, meaning most men can easily overpower most women in any given circumstance. So consider the inherent sense of vulnerability that imbalance engenders. Think about the idea (and I am talking to men at the moment) of living in a world where you are simply powerless to protect your most intimate possession, your body. Or how you would feel if half the population possessed the physical prowess to force themselves upon you in an instant. It's a terrifying prospect for women made worse when it becomes reality, which is why sex offenses take such a lasting toll on the victims who experience it.

And this crime was no exception.

Because after the officer had her trapped inside the room, he was relentless. She fought to keep him from peeling off her pants, and then her bra. But his strength was overwhelming.

Needless to say, you can guess what happened next. The officer, his gun belt hung over the bed, raped her. His final unspeakable act recounted solely by her mother.

The girl, the child, simply broke down and sobbed.

It's not a reaction you ever get used to. Dead bodies, maybe. Grieving mothers, sort of. But the pain of a child, never. And there's nothing really that can prepare you for it.

Her mother embraced her, a full body hug. A parental blanket draped over the anguish that was at that moment uncontrollable. An outpouring of grief that cascaded into visceral agony as my pen idled over my notebook.

At that point, the remaining details of the case didn't seem to matter. I finished the narrative on autopilot, faithfully documenting the remaining facts. How he dropped his pants, raped her, and abruptly disengaged when her friend pounded on the door to alert them her father was home. How she quickly dressed, bolted out of the room and down the stairs. How the cop followed her and the father stood in the living room speechless but unsure what to do.

When she was done, I thanked them both. I also made a promise, that regardless of the uniform her assailant was wearing that he would pay for his crime. I told her I would do everything in my power to get to the bottom of this case. And I would have an answer soon. They left quietly, their sorrow muted by the dull institutional colors and faltering fluorescent lights of the interrogation room.

The officer was summoned to district headquarters. As he sat in the chair waiting to answer my questions his nonchalance was as maddening as the crime itself. He seemed truly unconcerned. Almost aloof, even bored. I was stunned.

He was a bit disheveled. Like he had just rolled out of bed. And as I started the interrogation, he was initially just as careless with his answers. He admitted to asking for coffee, the conversation, but the sex, no. At least not at first. He feigned ignorance. I've seen it before, it's called the "Who, me?" act. A series of "What are you talking about?" responses. In his case, they were almost glib. Like he was going to play stupid throughout the interview. And if confronted fall back on his word, the man wearing a badge against the temperamental teen.

But of course, a man who conjures careless answers can be just as careless in other ways. And as I sat across from him engaging in a seemingly futile conversation, I noticed something on his uniform that was so surreal I still can't believe it.

There, on his pants, his police-issued uniform, was what appeared to be semen stains. Thats right, dried remains from what I assumed to be his criminal act with a teen girl. Evidence of a crime in plain sight. It was unreal. But also a chance to close the case and bring this man to account.

"I'm going to ask you a question," I started. "And I want you to think carefully about answering it." Again he proffered his dumb as a rock expression. "Did you change your pants recently? They look dirty."

He glanced down. I saw a glimmer of recognition in his eyes, even surprise. Yes, he'd played thick until now, but I don't think it took him very long to connect my question to the conspicuous evidence.

He dropped his head towards his pants as if he was contemplating just how profoundly stupid he was. Probably pondering how he could have forgotten to change after work. But even at this unquestionably incriminating moment, the man didn't lack for gall.

"It wasn t my fault," he offered weakly. "It was consensual." I didn t respond or interrupt him. I simply waited. I wanted to see just how much he would say.

"She wanted it; it wasn't just me."

Honestly, I wasn't surprised. He was not the first man I'd ever heard rationalize a criminal sex act. I sort of wished at that moment that I could force him to sit and watch the tremors of pain convulse through the body of the girl he abused. I thought to myself, maybe he could explain to her distraught mother just how her daughter sought sex with a cop more than twice her age.

That would have been just. Not justice in the traditional sense, but just all the same.

"So, you're telling me she seduced you?"

"Sort of."

"And this all happened two days ago. While you were on duty?"

"Yes."

I could only shake my head. He had admitted to the crime, excuses aside. Regardless of his explanation, he had raped a girl while on duty. You can't have consensual sex with a teenager while in uniform.

I advised him to get a lawyer, then charged him with statutory rape. But in the 1970s prosecution of sex crimes was less vigorous, to say the least. The courts were admittedly too sympathetic to the perpetrators. So despite my belief that more serious charges were warranted, the officer plead guilty to committing a perverted act with a minor. He barely received jail time, though he did lose his job.

But the punishment truly did not fit the crime. It was a stunning miscarriage of justice. Yes, we had charged, convicted him, and took his badge, but I do not think justice was served in this case.

Perhaps the only productive outcome of the entire ordeal was what I learned about policing and human nature, and to a certain extent how to deal with both when things go wrong. An assessment which gave me an indelible sense of just how important it is to hold cops accountable.

To be fair, a vast majority of the police officers I have worked with during my career are honest and upright individuals. Men and women who swear to uphold the law and promise to risk their lives in doing so. A group that is selfless, professional, and duty-bound by default.

Which is why I found the nonchalance of the cop so troubling. His cavalier attitude about the crime made a permanent impression upon me. I couldn't understand why he had been so careless about the evidence on his uniform. Or his matter-of-fact explanation that the victim had enticed him after he was caught dead to rights. Until I really thought about it, the implications of his apathy were not readily apparent.

But eventually, it hit home. That is, just how dangerous the power of policing could be in the wrong hands. And just how easy it is to be intoxicated with the public deference and to a certain extent hero worship that comes with the job. And how a bad cop could rationalize his or her actions regardless of circumstance.

Remember, this cop was a neighborhood 'officer friendly.' A man the people he served supposedly trusted. He was treated with great deference and given wide latitude. And yet it seemed to me the community's goodwill was used by this officer as a license to misbehave. And that's the flipside of mythologizing policing: some officers will simply be intoxicated by it. They'll be drunk with power. In other words, human, all too human.

To be honest, this revelation, while obviously naive, scared me. I realized we, meaning police, don't always grasp the extraordinary implications of the power—both legal and social—the community confers upon us. We perceive the ability to detain, arrest, and investigate as simple tools of the trade. But we never stop to consider just how profound and remarkable it is that we have them.

That's why the words trust and policing are so often used in tandem, but not fully fathomed. I realized then and there that for the public to trust us, we have to be vigilant about the use and occasional misuse of our constitutional privileges. We had to acknowledge as officers of the court that the power to impede freedom is a privilege—not a right. And that the combination of that privilege mixed with the unpredictable predilections of human nature could be dangerous without proper oversight and continued vigilance.

Which is why that day I made a pledge to myself to work towards not just holding my fellow officers accountable, but to advocate for and participate in their training. In a sense, I wanted to make sure I never had to sit across the table again from an officer so far afield from the calling. I wanted to instill in every cop I worked with a deep respect for the law.

So I worked vigilantly to improve my understanding of it, and devised programs uniquely tailored to improve testimony in court and the process of writing search and seizure warrants. It became, in essence, my *raison d'etre* for being a cop. I felt then, and still do now, that there is a better way to police. A process for law enforcement outlined in the underlying principles of the U.S. Constitution that, if followed, can produce better results.

Remember, the framers of the Constitution were skeptical of state power. They constructed the document to preserve individual rights, and they did this long before professional policing emerged. It's a concept easy to forget amid violence and chaos. Principles easy to abandon when your life and property are threatened. But without it, policing is less of a profession and more an exercise in vigilantism.

Which is why I have written two books not just on the cases or the crimes I investigated, but the lessons I learned about policing in the process. And one of the most important is that there are no conditional shortcuts to being a good cop. Any expediencies, both legal and strategic, invoked in the name of safety or fear will produce neither. Any compromise of our civil liberties and intrinsic rights to ameliorate threats both real and imagined will only serve to diminish the community we pledge to protect.

And these same lessons apply to policing ourselves. The truth is that being a cop entails confronting the contradictions and often harsh realities of need to be safe and free daily. It is our job to walk the high wire balance between civil liberties and personal safety. As much as policing is portrayed as simplistic and brutal, it is a precarious balancing act. A tedious and inherently risky process made more fraught when officers break the law.

So my final thoughts in The Book of Cop are this:

Policing is not as simple as it seems. Cops are just as human as the people they serve. And crime, just like any human behavior, is endlessly complex. It is as natural as any other tendency or trait. And it must be dealt with in a way that brings the least harm to all, particularly our civil liberties and our fragile but vibrant democracy.

We are conjoined by this task in ways we do not want to admit. Not police on one side and civilians on the other, but a community which must survive and hopefully thrive together. That is the most difficult reality of policing to grasp. There is no 'us' against 'them' in a functional democracy. There are no simple enemies or unimpeachable cops. There are human beings who wear the badge and human beings who commit crimes and occasionally they are one and the same. A convoluted set of behaviors and institutions that cannot be reduced to simple narrative tropes like 'good' versus 'evil' or bad guys versus good.

The truth is our collective communal task is to find a balance between the need to eradicate crime and our desire to preserve the free and open society we all hopefully cherish. It is not an easy job. Nor is it a process that hews to the exhortations of the overly-simplistic rhetoric employed to sustain it. We should never, as a society, answer the call to 'support the police' blindly. Never give up our right to have a reasoned and transparent discussion on how we expect policing to work.

Criminality is not a permanent condition. It is a problem with many origins that must be addressed, but not at the expense of who we are. The point of policing is to mitigate criminality, not completely and unequivocally eliminate the risk of it. That means for our vibrant democracy to survive, the men and women who wear the badge must be open with and connected to the people they serve. And the public must feel empowered to define what it means to police, and how and why police exist at all.

I started this book with ruminations on the principles espoused by the former British Prime Minister Sir Robert Peele. One of his most pertinent and I believe substantive charges was this: to recognize always that the test of police efficiency is the absence of crime and disorder and not the visible evidence of police action in dealing with them.

In other words, the success of policing is not measured by the presence of tactical units in bulletproof vests and baseball caps, swat teams draped in Kevlar, or a slew of statistic producing traffic stops. The best measure of our success is the ability to have the most substantive impact on crime without interfering with the general quality of life of the people we serve.

Its a goal, to say the least, that is both tricky and endlessly complicated. The only thing I know for sure is that the best way to achieve it is together. A community united cognizant that fighting crime is never simple, and that the battle against it involves us all.

CHAPTER TEN:
TALKING TRUISMS

Since I retired, I've felt duty bound not just to share my past experiences, but to speak out against what I believe are misconceptions and half-truths about law enforcement in this country.

During the uprising in the aftermath of the death of Freddie Gray in police custody, that apparent lack of understanding was acute. Rumours that police had stopped doing their job and crime was rising as a consequence abounded. And the idea that overly-aggressive tactics were the only way to fight crime became political currency for police unions and their advocates.

So to set the record straight, I gave a series of interviews on some of the most egregious assumptions to my co-writer Stephen Janis. I thought the ideas we discussed were not just relevant to the topic of this book, but worth documenting so that the ongoing discussion about policing has some context.

Below are the unabridged transcripts of those interviews, which I hope will add some substantive perspective to idea of just how we should police cities like Baltimore and beyond.

STEPHEN JANIS, INVESTIGATIVE REPORTER, TRNN: Hello. My name is Stephen Janis, and I'm an investigative reporter for The Real News Network in Baltimore.

Once again, Baltimore finds itself in the middle of a stretch of unrelenting violence. With 35 murders so far in May, the city is on track to have one of its most deadly months since 1999. And so far homicides are up 40 percent over last year. Along with these killings are calls for police to respond. In fact, the cry for more police, more jails, and more law enforcement has been the mantra of Baltimore for decades. But despite the fact that we have one of the largest police departments, and spending for policing far outweighs schools and recreation centers, there's little evidence that it works. And therein lies the dilemma. Why do we keep turning to police when it doesn't seem to work, and what are we missing about the limits of policing and the criminal justice system in the face of evidence that our solutions may be misguided? Here to help me answer that question is a man who worked the streets of Baltimore during one of its most violent decades in its history. During the decade of the 1970s, Baltimore experienced roughly 300 murders a year. It was the job of our next guest, Lt. Stephen Tabeling, to solve many of those cases. Since then he has written a book with me, full disclosure, called You Can't Stop Murder. Part of its premise is that this idea that policing can solve complex social problems is flawed and may even be making the situation worse. Mr. Tabeling, thank you for joining us.

JANIS: Well, explain to us, we're looking at an extremely violent month. And part of the thing people say, we need more police, we need more cops on the street, we need more policing. But you say that's not the only part of this problem, and you have the premise that you can't stop murder. What did you mean by that?

TABELING: Well, I don't think you need more police. You need more experienced people. You need to have people that know what they're doing when they're investigating, and you can't use committees to investigate crimes. You have to have experienced investigators. And I go back to my time. Investigators used to go out on crime scenes by themselves. And then if it come time for an arrest, then we would call uniformed officers.

When I was there, we had 28 men in homicide and we had over 300 murders a year. I could send any one of those investigators out and feel comfortable that he was going to do the right job. So it never took more than two on a crime scene to come up with a solution to a crime.

JANIS: One of the premises is that in modern policing, in contemporary policing, you can prevent murders. But you say that's kind of a flawed philosophy or flawed idea. What do you mean by that, you can't stop murder?

TABELING: You can't stop murder. In our book we said that. Murder is a crime of passion. You're not going to stop it. But can you do some things that can help to prevent it, absolutely. When you have good investigations and are swift, and people are convicted. And one of the things that bothers me is stop and frisk. That's one of the greatest tools police every got, and I don't think they're properly trained. And if you look at New York, murders went down, what, 60 percent when they were using stop and frisk because people that carried guns knew that the possibility of them getting stopped was going to be there. So when they stopped talking to people and stopping people, they didn't care about carrying weapons.

JANIS: But the city of Baltimore arrested 100,000 people a year. 100,000 people a year. And the homicide rate went up. So how can stop and frisk or any of these policies in policing really prevent murders or really stop--.

TABELING: Let's take a look at the 100,000 people they arrested. What were they charged with? Did they get any weapons, they were corner arrests, they were disorderly conducts. They were people on the porch drinking beer. It was the broken windows syndrome, low tolerance. Most of those people, they probably shouldn't have been arrested. They weren't quality arrests. They were numbers.See, so when you start getting into the areas where there's a lot of crime, where there's a lot of weapons, you have to have a way to get those weapons off of the street. And one of the best ways--look, the case Terry v. Ohio came out from the Supreme Court in an eight to one decision. And the Supreme Court said if a police officer knows a person is violent in a neighborhood of high activity, and that officer has articulable reasonable suspicion to suspect that person is armed he has the right to detain and pat the person down. But the problem is you have to be properly trained, and you have to know when and how and to evaluate when to stop people. And then when you go to court you have to be able to testify from your training and your experience exactly why you did what you did.

JANIS: But even in the case of New York, with stop and frisk, it was determined that it was racially biased. And similarly with zero tolerance, they're both accused of being racially biased. So how can you say they're effective if they're not being administered justly?

TABELING: Let's take a look at racially biased. I work in a western district. I'm a white police officer. It's a predominantly black neighborhood. There's a lot of killings in that neighborhood, there's a lot of robberies. Who am I going to be stopping? What am I going to be looking for? It's the same if you take a black officer and send him to East Baltimore, and he's going to be doing the same kind of operation. Who's he going to be stopping? And really, don't you think whatever neighborhoods you go in, you're doing these things to protect the people who live in these neighborhoods. That's my whole thing about that.

JANIS: Well, let me ask you another--there was a story in the Sun over the weekend about how the union's contract had prevented the improvements in policing. How many people did you have in homicide when there were 300 murders a year compared to today? You had very few, much--.

TABELING: Twenty-eight.

JANIS: Twenty-eight people.

TABELING: Yes.

JANIS: So how is it possible that we have 60 or 70, and we have a lower closure rate today than we had 30, 40 years ago?

TABELING: A lot of reasons. Lack of experience. We've lost the technique of interrogation. Of, we have officers with no imagination. You've got to have an imagination, you've got to think things through. You just have to have a way of, I'm going to say profile, but not profile on a person. Profile in crimes and crime scenes, and that can give you an idea who committed a crime. We don't have the street smart people that we used to have. Let's get foot patrol back in there. I can remember the days when I was working in Homicide. If I had a nickname of a guy, got the post officer, he'd pull a book out of his pocket. He'd say oh yeah, this is where he live--they don't do that now. They've got no responsibility for anything on the streets. Listen, your backbone is your uniformed police officers. And who's the least trained? The patrol officer out on the street. What he does can go all the way to the United States Supreme Court and it can break your case. And I'll guarantee you if you talk to the State's Attorney they'll tell you that they're hesitant about putting the first officer on the scene on the witness stand.

JANIS: I mean, in the age of technology when this should be easier, we have a larger police department with more investigators, and you can't achieve a closure rate. I mean, is the union, is the problem that there's not enough accountability with police in the sense that they have too much power, maybe?

TABELING: I'm going to go back, again. It's a lack of training, it's a lack of experience, and I gave you this example before and it's in the book. When I was in a police academy just three or four years ago, we had a program that was first ever in the history of law schools where we actually did trials at the University of Baltimore with judges and attorneys. First time in the history of law school. And the judges on circuit court said this is the best program they've ever seen. And the State's Attorney said we are not afraid to put the first officer on the scene because they know how to testify. I left the academy and they stopped doing it.

JANIS: Well, that raises a big question. Why would they stop training officers to be able to testify in court, and why would they stop teaching the law in general?

TABELING: It's a lot of work. It's a lack of experience. When I did that training--.

JANIS: Well, just stop you there. You say it's a lot of work. What do you mean, it's a lot of work?

TABELING: Well first of all, I bring a class of 50 people in and I'd have to write scenarios on burglaries, armed robberies, and all kind of problems and split the class up in groups of four. Talk to them every morning. You have to write a report. You have to interview a witness. You have to interrogate a suspect. You have to write a search and seizure warrant. And I had to, I'd say spoon feed them. Because I'd take--I'd come to work every morning at 6:00. And I'd get these groups in there. And then when they got their folders right, then we would go to a State's Attorney, and the State's Attorney would go over it. I have tapes of all this. I have tapes of what happened up at the University of Baltimore. One of the most important things is, Steve, anybody can make an arrest, but anybody can't carry that case through to convict some body in a court of law. And that's where a lot of it's lacking.

JANIS: But you're talking about an entirely different type of policing. I mean, what's taught in the academy recently, or at least the past seven or eight years is more aggressive, physical training. What's been taught, what we saw with the Freddie Gray case was people chasing people around the neighborhood without too much--without probable cause. Why has policing changed so much in the past 40 years? What has changed it?

TABELING: Well, nobody listen, but I'll keep on saying it. It's a lack of legal training and understanding the 4th, 5th, and 6th amendments to the Constitution. It's a lack of being able to go out on that street and when you make an arrest, evaluate what you're doing. You go out there and it happens how, that's it. Make a decision, just like that. And if you don't have something up here to do it, it's going to be very difficult.

JANIS: Okay. Now, we're looking at this situation, 35 murders this month so far. You're police commissioner, you're working the Baltimore City Police Department. How do you respond to that?

TABELING: Well first of all, I'm going to look at who's in my homicide squad and I'm going to look at my commanders. And I don't micromanage my people. Every time I look at a homicide scene I see majors and colonels and everybody else out on the street. You can't micromanage. That shows me that they don't have any trust in their investigators, and I doubt if any of those commanders know how to do a homicide.So you can't put people in that position that you're looking over their shoulder all--you're practically telling these guys, you don't know what you're doing. So take a look around. In this department, we have sergeants with three and four years' service. We have lieutenants with seven and eight year. And I think majors don't have too much more time.

JANIS: So what did it used to be?

TABELING: It used to be when I made sergeants, you had to be a patrolman for five years. And if you made sergeant in seven or eight years you were doing a good thing. Once you made lieutenant you had to wait two years to take the test. You never made it in two years because we had a seniority system. I hear from a lot of the people I taught in the academy, will tell me that they'll go to a lieutenant or a sergeant in the street and they can't get an answer. That's bad, that's your middle--that's your people out on the street. You have to be able to answer questions for people.

JANIS: Is that politics? I mean, what

TABELING: Listen. In this city of Baltimore, we've had I don't know how many police commissioners that come from out of town, and they try to make us their department. This is a unique city, and it's been told a lot, this is a city of villages. It's a different understanding. Here's what you have to do. If I was police commissioner, people would be out of those cars. There'd be foot patrol. I don't care, it costs a lot of money, but that's what I would do. Because that's one of the things that keeps crime down, is having cops on foot out there.

JANIS: One of the things people have been saying is because of the Freddie Gray incident police have been slowing down. But they're public servants. And do you believe, number one, that they are slowing down, and do you believe that's justified?

TABELING: Well, I don't--listen, I'm one guy. I don't believe it's justified, but let's look at it both ways. If I'm a police officer, and say I make a mistake on a probable cause issue and the case goes to court. The judge does what? He dismisses the guy. In a situation like we have now, say those officers made a mistake, they got charged. And you've got police officers out there now saying wait a minute. If I put my hands on this guy and I make a mistake, I'm afraid I'm going to jail.

JANIS: But even though they're committing a crime, shouldn't everyone be subject to the same type of law that you talk about?

TABELING: Everybody should, and everybody should be doing their job. And listen, I guarantee you 98 or 99 percent of the police out there are good cops. You've got that one or two percent to drag us all down. Listen, you know that I've locked up policemen. I'm not proud of it. And I know what they are, and I also know that the good men don't get treated right.

JANIS: But why don't the good people speak up more? If they're good. I mean, this assumption, we say everyone's good, there's only a few bad. Why don't they speak up? Why don't they--because, why don't they prevent this?

TABELING: Because they're afraid they're going to lose their job. Because they're afraid they don't have any backing. They're afraid the police commissioner and the mayor won't back them up. You make a mistake when you make an arrest, a police officer shouldn't get arrested. If he makes a mistake and it goes to court and the judge dismisses it, that's the way to--now, if--.

JANIS: But what if someone dies as a result? Like Freddie--.

TABELING: You've got a whole other set of circumstances. You're asking me now why the cops don't want to--.

JANIS: Right, I understand.

TABELING: So the cops don't want to do anything because they're afraid if they make a mistake then they're going to get charged. And when you're out there on those streets, believe me, you never know what you're going to run into. Every call is different and you've got to be on your toes all the time. Now, these cops now all over the United States, they're a little bit jittery now. And another policeman got shot in Mississippi, another policeman got shot in Louisiana, another police officer got shot in New Mexico, and another one got beat up. So it's going all over the country, and these guys are, these guys are getting a little bit upset.

JANIS: I'm sorry, I'm interrupting. Go ahead. But ultimately, you know, the law--I guess your idea was that the law is the best thing we have in terms of--yeah.

TABELING: Absolutely. The thing that I see is, you're bringing people in to become police officers. Before they come in, or truck drivers, or mailmen, they might be a lot of things. I've had accountants and everything else come in. they know absolutely nothing about the law, and they're going to be the people out on the street. You have to give them something to take out there with them so that they can make decisions. You've got a program in college called a criminal justice degree. I've had people in my class in the police academy that when I was giving them instruction they'd say, why don't they give us this in college? It seems to me, just my own opinion, that the last thing they think of, the last thing they think of, is the law. Look at that $250,000 survey that they did for the Baltimore Police Department. How many sentences in that survey talks about training? Not many. Maybe it's a paragraph or something. I just, it's just me, I've been around with this since 1954. And as a private investigator I've been back and see what policemen do on the kind of investigations that they do. And then you go back and say, supervision. Supervision, and the supervisors aren't properly trained. So I put something on the internet. I said I'd like to have the opportunity to bring all the command staff in and give them a test.

EXCERPT FROM THE STORY: Former Baltimore Cop: You Can't Enforce the Law by Breaking It

STEPHEN JANIS, INVESTIGATIVE REPORTER, TRNN: Hello. My name is Stephen Janis. I'm an investigative reporter for The Real News Network in Baltimore.

In the wake of indictment of six officers for the in-custody death of Freddie Gray, it's not just the city police department that's feeling the heat. A recent article in the Baltimore Sun reports that officers feel constrained by intense scrutiny, and with it implications of violence in a city that is still plagued by one of the highest homicide rates in the country will be harder to fight. It's an all-too-common refrain in the era of contemporary policing that says the law and policing by the book is an impediment to fighting crime in cities like Baltimore.

But is it true? Is combating violence and policing by the law too incompatible concepts? Well, our next guest says no. In fact, he's written a book about it and argues that following the law not only leads to better outcomes on the street, but is the best way to reduce crime. The book, You Can't Stop Murder, of which I am a co-author, explores Stephen Tabeling premise through actual cases. In fact, some of the most notorious murder cases in city history. Stephen Tabeling is a former homicide lieutenant and a former police chief. Thank you for joining us, Mr. Tabeling. I appreciate it.

STEPHEN TABELING, FMR. BALTIMORE CITY HOMICIDE LT.: You're welcome.

JANIS: So this idea that aggressive policing is somehow constrained by the law. Talk about the law, and how the law actually can work for policing.

TABELING: Well, I think that police officers should know the law, especially the 4th, 5th, and 6th Amendments of the United States Constitution. I think that more emphasis should be placed on patrol officers to know the law, because they're in on--any kind of crime that you can name, they're first on the scene. If they don't know the law, they can make a mistake and a whole case is gone. And just remember, what that little cop does on the street can go all the way to the United States Supreme Court. And not only that. If they understand the concepts of those amendments that I just mentioned, when they're on the street they're better able to evaluate a crime, they're better able to evaluate when and why they can make an arrest. And then they're more capable of articulating that reason for arrest when they get in a court of law. We had some programs in a police academy where we went all the way through court testimony. We had a court judge from circuit court, we had prosecutors, we had defense attorneys, and we had law students. And it turned out to be one of the best programs ever. But don't ask me why, they stopped it. And my understanding from the University of Baltimore law school, that was the first time in the history of the law school that anything like that had ever been done. But just think, the 4th Amendment. You know, search and seizure, individual rights. The 5th Amendment, it talks about a person's right to, not to talk to you. The 6th Amendment gives you the right to an attorney. Now, if you know those amendments, all these laws are not an impediment to you because you better understand them. There's a bad understanding of Miranda. A lot of police officers don't really understand Miranda. Let's take, for example, stop and frisk. You know, that's the best tool that police have ever been handed by the Supreme Court. It came out in an eight to one decision, and what the Supreme Court said in that case is if an officer knows that someone's on the street and are presently armed and dangerous to themselves or society, should a police officer shrug his shoulders, or should we give him a tool? And they gave us a tool. And it's called articulable, reasonable suspicion. But unfortunately what happens a lot of times when the officers don't know exactly that law, sometimes they'll be patting people down illegally. They'll make mistakes. But give them the tools. And I've always been an advocate for the law. And not for lawyer law. I mean for practical application of law on the street, because what's an officer looking for? Probable cause, probability based on his training and experience that this person committed a crime. If you get too many lawyers involved, they're looking for moral certainty when you arrest somebody, and it doesn't always work that way.

JANIS: Well, looking at what we're hearing, we see this article that says, well, because of some of the constraints we don't feel like we can go out there and do our jobs. Violence is going to increase. We can't stop it. But you kind of made the opposite argument in your book. I mean, is that really true?

TABELING: Well, it's no constraints--I think the law has made better police officers. But think about the constraints on these police today. It's command. It's command. It's not the police themselves. And they're really, you know, from what I can understand, is really upset. And I understand there could be a lot of resignations coming in, because the officers are so disgusted. But let's get back. The law is, in my opinion, is the most important thing that you can have. When you know the law, you're going to be a better police officer. When all those laws start coming out in the '60s they said oh, we're handcuffed. No you're not. There's a lot of legal things that you can do with these laws. But you have to know what you're doing. You have to be properly trained in the law. And I can tell you this. And I'll bet this. I can go in most police departments and write on the blackboard 4, 5, and 6, the Amendments, and say to them, what do these amendments mean to you? You know how many answers I'll really get? And I'm not just saying this to say it. I've experienced it. I've given tests in it. So I think we've got to concentrate more on that law concept.

JANIS: Well, how does that--I mean, Baltimore City Police Department in the past decade or so has used very aggressive tactics. You know, disrupt tactics. You know, go out onto a corner, disrupt, harass people. In the neighborhood of Freddie Gray they said they're constantly coming up and telling them to move on, or do--how does that jive with your idea of policing and your idea of the law?

TABELING: Well, that doesn't jive with my idea of the law. You've got to have a reason to stop somebody. But just think about this, too. A person that has committed crimes in the past is going to knock the police at every chance that they get. I'm not saying police don't do that. But what I'm saying is some of these people that have been arrested in the past, they probably don't like police. And they'll tell you about the harassment. Yes, some of it. But to listen to some of these people that's been in before, it's--I don't think it's quite as bad as what they say it is.

JANIS: But you have a department that illegally arrested tens of thousands of people. How can we trust anything they say at this point?

TABELING: Well, trust has to be built back up with the police department. And I think, I think the whole thing starts in the police academy. I haven't been there since late 2009, and I can tell you that some of the programs that I have--they've done away with. I mean, University of Baltimore would love to see that program come back again. It was--.

JANIS: That was the program that was the--.

TABELING: The court testimony. Because here's what we did. The officer knew, had to know how to write a report. Interview, interrogate, write search and seizure warrants, and get on the witness stand and testify. And prior to his trial at the University of Baltimore, we sit him down with State's Attorneys, went over the case, took the whole process of how it would go through. I don't know what they're doing now. But I've watched police testify, and that's one of the reasons why they lose cases, is because they really don't know how to testify.

JANIS: You told me a couple--almost a year before all this stuff happened, you went to the Mayor with a proposal. You and some retired officers. Talk about that a little bit.

TABELING: Well, I didn't go, but some people from the retired association who I, that I know are very capable people. A couple of them are retired majors. And through our retired association we made a, we told the Mayor that we would do a survey of the department. And it wouldn't cost anything, we wanted to do it because we were concerned with what's happening in the department. And as far as I know, the people that made that approach have never got anything back. The story we hear, hearsay, we don't want any old dinosaurs coming in here and telling us what to do. What do those old-timers know? Well, we've made several approaches to do training. Look, I've made another approach. You know, I had a meeting to do training, and that's been almost a year ago. I'm still waiting for a telephone call. They hired a law firm now, $50,000 to do a program. Come on, let's get some people in there who really know what they're doing.

JANIS: So I mean, the concern was what, specifically, with the retired-- what did you think was wrong with the department?

TABELING: Well, we didn't like--we didn't like the way that the police were operating. The way that they were writing reports. Their lack of knowledge of the law. And yeah, they were arresting people without any probable cause. And we were concerned about that. And we were concerned--we were concerned because it wasn't the officer's fault all the time, because they weren't properly trained. If they're not properly trained and don't know what to do, you, how are you going to blame them? Look, when you're a police officer on the street, it's no waiting. It's instantaneous. You get a call, you go. That's it. And now you're stuck with that. And if you don't have anything up here to deal with that, you've got yourself a problem. It's an instantaneous operation, but you've got to be trained for it properly. And believe me, it sticks here if it's put in here.

JANIS: There's been a lot of controversy about the charges of the officer in the Freddie Gray case. I'm not going to ask you to comment on that directly. But one of the things I thought I understood is that when you take someone into custody, what are your legal obligations to that person who's in your custody, once you handcuff them, or they're, you restrain them or whatever? What are your legal obligations as a police officer?

TABELING: Well, when the person in your custody you have to take care of them. I mean, you try to treat them as easy as you can. If they need any hospitalization you take them to the hospital. You do everything humanly possible for them. And you always teach officers, you never hit a man with handcuffs for anything like that. But you know, there are times when you're going to have to protect yourself. When you protect yourself if it comes to the point where you might have to hit somebody and they go down, that's the end of it. You don't start after a person's down because then what do you get into? You get into brutality. Everyone's not going to go with you willingly. There's going to be a time in a policeman's career where somebody's going to hit him and he's going to have to protect himself. But again, there's limitations to what you do with that.

JANIS: So you served this department for most of your career. You have watched it change. Was training, and was the kind of things you talk about, could that have prevented the mess that we see now? I mean, let's face it, they are under three investigations simultaneously. That's almost unprecedented. Could the type of [incompre.] really fix policing in a city like Baltimore?

TABELING: Well, I just happen to think--I happen to think training is the answer. I think that there has to be more emphasis on the law. There has to be more scenario-based training. There has to be less, less emphasis on physical training. You have to have physical training because you have to know how to take care of yourself. You have to know how to shoot a gun. But I think there's limitations, that physical education shouldn't dominate a police academy.

JANIS: Last question. You know, we have talked about this idea of your book, and we both discuss this at length, You Can't Stop Murder. And in terms of police and crime fighting, it sort of leads one to a different conclusion than the aggressive, get out in the streets, that investigations in lawful policing. Just explain that a little bit, what you mean by, you can't stop murder, in the sense--what it means for policing.

TABELING: Well, you really can't stop murder because murder is a crime of passion. You can put a cop on every corner, and somebody's going to get murdered. But what you can do, what you can do with good policing--and when you arrest somebody, you make a good arrest, and when they go to court you convict them. If you got somebody for murder and they walk out two and three times, what's the problem most of the time? It's a bad investigation. And don't you think these people don't look at this on the street? You know, to see what's happening. And you need swift, good prosecution of cases, and put the people away that belong away. And look at the people that are out on the street, that if it hadn't been a good investigation and they [inaud.] got convicted that they would have never been out on the street. But you can't stop murder, but you can do some preventive things to stop street-type murders and things like that.

And the preventive things are, is to do good investigations and get the bad people off of the street.

ABOUT THE AUTHORS

STEPHEN TABELING has been a cop for more than six decades, nearly half that time in Baltimore City alone, where he received 48 Commendations and six Bronze Stars for investigative work above and beyond the call of duty, retiring as a lieutenant. He began his career with the Baltimore Police Department in 1954. Following his retirement at the end of the turbulent 1970s he served as director of public safety for Johns Hopkins Hospital and later in the same position for Loyola University Maryland (the former Loyola College) for more than a decade. In the interim he was chief of police in the City of Salisbury, on Marylands Eastern Shore. In 2000 Tabeling was called back by the BPD to provide an analysis of its Homicide Squad, followed by nine years of recruit training for new police officers as well as in-service training for the departments veterans.

STEPHEN JANIS is an award-winning investigative journalist whose work has been acclaimed both in print and in television. As the Senior Investigative Reporter for the now defunct Baltimore Examiner, he won two Maryland DC Delaware Press Association Awards for his work on the number of unsolved murders in Baltimore and the killings of prostitutes. His in-depth work on the city's zero-tolerance policing policies garnered an NAACP President's Award. Later, he founded Investigative Voice, an award-winning website that is the subject of the upcoming documentary Fit To Print. As an Investigative Producer for WBFF/Fox 45, he has won three successive Capital Emmys: two for Best Investigative Series and one for Outstanding Historical/Cultural Piece.

As a composer and producer, Janis won two ASCAP Rhythm and Soul Awards for his production of several hip-hop classics, including Let Me Clear My Throat by DJ Kool, Biz Markie, and Doug E. Fresh. His production company Instant Records produced Hard Knock Life for Jay Z. Later, he co-wrote music with director John Waters for his film Cecil B Demented starring Melanie Griffith and Stephen Dorff. The film was a non-juried selection for the Cannes Film Festival. He is the author of two books on the philosophy of policing, Why Do We Kill? The Pathology of Murder in Baltimore and You Can't Stop Murder: Truths About Policing in Baltimore and Beyond. He has also written two novels, This Dream Called Death and Orange: The Diary of an Urban Surrealist. His teaches journalism at Towson University and taught digital culture at the Johns Hopkins University's Master's Program.